Ten Days That Shook the World of Education

Ten Days That Shook the World of Education

A Close Look at the People Who Facilitated Educational Change

Donald Parkerson and Jo Ann Parkerson

ROWMAN & LITTLEFIELD
Lanham • Boulder • New York • London

Published by Rowman & Littlefield
An imprint of The Rowman & Littlefield Publishing Group, Inc.
4501 Forbes Boulevard, Suite 200, Lanham, Maryland 20706
https://rowman.com

6 Tinworth Street, London SE11 5AL, United Kingdom

Copyright © 2021 by The Rowman & Littlefield Publishing Group, Inc.

All rights reserved. No part of this book may be reproduced in any form or by any electronic or mechanical means, including information storage and retrieval systems, without written permission from the publisher, except by a reviewer who may quote passages in a review.

British Library Cataloguing in Publication Information Available

Library of Congress Cataloging-in-Publication Data

Names: Parkerson, Donald Hugh, author. | Parkerson, Jo Ann, author.
Title: Ten days that shook the world of education : a close look at the people who facilitated educational change / Donald Parkerson and Jo Ann Parkerson.
Description: Lanham, Maryland : Rowman & Littlefield, 2021. | Includes bibliographical references.
Identifiers: LCCN 2020048170 (print) | LCCN 2020048171 (ebook) | ISBN 9781475852349 (cloth) | ISBN 9781475852356 (paperback) | ISBN 9781475852363 (epub)
Subjects: LCSH: Education--United States--History. | Educational equalization--United States--History. | Educators--United States--Biography.
Classification: LCC LA205 .P37 2021 (print) | LCC LA205 (ebook) | DDC 370.973--dc23
LC record available at https://lccn.loc.gov/2020048170

To those who Shook the World of Education

Contents

Acknowledgments ix

Introduction xi

1. Jean-Jacques Rousseau—The Philosophy of Modern Education: Spring 1762 — 1
2. Joseph Lancaster—Teaching the Poor: January 1, 1798 — 15
3. Emma Willard—Women's Education: September 7, 1821 — 29
4. Horace Mann—Father of the Common School: June 29, 1837 — 43
5. William McGuffey—The Graded *Reader*: April 1, 1836 — 61
6. John Dewey—Father of Progressive Education: January 13, 1896 — 77
7. W. E. B. Du Bois—Equality of African American Education: January 1, 1903 — 91
8. Horace Mann Bond—A Challenge to Standardized Testing: March 1, 1924 — 105
9. Thurgood Marshall—The End of Legal Segregation: May 17, 1954 — 121
10. The Kids are All Right—Political Activism: February 14, 2018 — 135

Conclusion 149

References 155

About the Authors 159

Acknowledgments

We wish to thank our family, friends, and colleagues for their support and encouragement, especially Cindy Ripperger; Gonzalo Soruco; Chris Oakley, chair of the History Department; and Dean Allison Danell. We also appreciate the generous endorsement of our book by Dr. Allen Guidry and Dr. Shelly Wilburn.

Tom Koerner, senior editor at Rowman & Littlefield, provided formative and provocative feedback, and the associate editor Carlie Wall and the production editor were extremely helpful.

Introduction

Certain moments in American history have been seared into our collective consciousness either from our study of the past or our own personal experience. Whether it was July 4, 1776, when the Founding Fathers signed the Declaration of Independence and set the United States on a new path toward an experiment in democracy or July 20, 1969, when members of *Apollo 11* landed on the moon and brought the world to the threshold of space exploration for the first time in human history.

Other moments were more tragic. Many of us remember December 7, 1941, when Japan attacked the U.S. naval base at Pearl Harbor in Hawaii, triggering U.S. entry into World War II. We also recall November 22, 1963, a moment that stunned Americans with the assassination of the beloved President John F. Kennedy.

And of course who can forget the attack on America by al Qaeda terrorists on September 11, 2001, when the twin towers of the World Trade Center were destroyed, the Pentagon was damaged, and a handful of brave Americans on Flight 93 thwarted an attack planned for the White House by crashing their aircraft into a barren field near Shanksville, Pennsylvania.

While these and dozens of other events have changed the course of American history, we typically ignore the critical moments that transformed U.S. educational history. *Ten Days That Shook the World of Education* seeks to address some of these critical moments that changed the course of our unique educational experiment.

These important incidents center on how everyday people did extraordinary things to challenge injustice and facilitate educational change. Whether it was Joseph Lancaster's opening of his Boroughs Road School for the poor children of industrial workers, Emma Willard's female academy, or Thurgood Marshall's success as chief NAACP consul in the Supreme Court school desegregation decision of Brown v. *Board of Education*, the human spirit challenged existing injustices and "shook" the world of education.

Ten Days also recognizes the importance of external forces such as the Industrial and Market Revolutions; the growing recognition of individual rights in American society, including those of women, African Americans, and other social and cultural minorities; as well as the need for school safety in an era of growing gun violence.

Here, for example, we center our attention on the response to the disruptions of society by the forces of industrial change by the progressive John Dewey, the challenge of full educational opportunities for African Americans by W. E. B Du Bois, and the grassroots movement for responsible gun control legislation by the kids at Parkland's Marjory Stoneman Douglas High School.

By centering our attention on everyday people who have faced seemingly insurmountable problems in our society and then acted to challenge them, we offer a more concrete and personal perspective of how educational change happens.

First, we turn to Jean-Jacques Rousseau, who provided the fundamental philosophical basis of modern child-centered education.

JEAN-JACQUES ROUSSEAU—THE PHILOSOPHY OF MODERN EDUCATION

Spring 1762

The world of education had remained virtually unchanged for a millennium until eighteenth-century "Enlightenment scholars" such as Jean-Jacques Rousseau, John Locke, Denis Diderot, and others challenged the Judeo-Christian vision of humankind. That perception of the basic sinful nature of man, who had been corrupted by "original sin," was recounted in the Bible and had become the guiding principle of education in Western society.

But it wasn't until Jean-Jacques Rousseau integrated these Enlightenment ideas that we saw a fundamental challenge to the basic Christian orthodoxy of education. Rousseau argued that children were not "wicked" and sinful and in need of severe discipline to shape their values and become useful members of society. For Rousseau, they were essentially good and could be molded by proper education.

Earlier John Locke had argued that children came into this world not tainted by the sins of their fathers but as a kind of tabula rasa, a blank slate, what he referred to as "white paper, void of all character" that could then be scripted through education. These ideas were reinforced by other Enlightenment scholars who challenged the traditional Judeo-Christian vision of humankind's innate depravity.

Abbe de Saint Pierre, for example, in his famous work *Observations on the Continuous Progress of Reason* in 1732 contended that human progress was possible through scientific and rational thought and not exclusively through the divine auspices of the church.

Other enlightenment figures also challenged the fundamental ideas of the church concerning human development. Voltaire, for example, rejected the teachings of the Bible and argued that individuals were responsible for their own actions and could achieve enlightenment through reason and education.

But the world of education was shaken to its foundation in the spring of 1762 when Jean-Jacques Rousseau published two works that challenged both the Judeo-Christian position on progress as well as its established ideas on education.

In his *The Social Contract*, published in April of that year, Rousseau grappled with the question of how to create an interdependent society and community in the face of growing individualism and market interests. This question would continue to perplex scholars for the next century and would be reassessed by John Dewey in the early twentieth century.

The Social Contract opened with a classic quote that challenged the accepted vision of the wickedness of mankind emanating from original sin. Rousseau wrote, "Man is born free and everywhere he is in chains." Here Rousseau criticized traditional society because it restricted human freedom and essentially created inequality. In his view, individuals were born pure but were corrupted by society. In short, while *The Social Contract* was important in inspiring reforms and revolutionary activity of the late eighteenth and nineteenth centuries, it also opened the door to educational reform.

In his second book published in May 1762, *Emile, or On Education*, Rousseau applied his philosophical ideas of the goodness of man to education. Rousseau was proud of this work and once referred to it as "the best and most important of all his writings." In *Emile* he emphasized the importance of producing well-balanced, open-minded individuals who would develop naturally without the impositions and restrictions of society.

While traditional forms of education typically perceived children as essentially malicious and therefore the role of education was to subordinate them to a higher authority, Rousseau argued that they were inherently good and the role of education was to allow a child's natural curiosity to guide learning. Rousseau's new detailed educational plan established the "romantic" vision of education that would inspire generations of democratically oriented educators from Johann Pestalozzi and Horace Mann to later reformers such as John Dewey and many others.

The publication of the philosophical tract *The Social Contract* followed by his educational novel *Emile*, in the spring of 1762, shook the world of education, set a course that challenged traditional forms of education, and helped foster new ideas of the modern school.

JOSEPH LANCASTER—TEACHING THE POOR

January 1, 1798

While the philosophical basis of education was slowly changing, and more and more scholars saw the necessity of a new perspective on learning, few considered the importance of teaching the poor. For the most part, education was the province of the rich and powerful. Its purpose was to train well-rounded gentlemen who would lead society and government.

But Joseph Lancaster was different. He shook the world of education by recognizing the need for poor children to receive an education. And through his own determination he opened schools for the poor throughout Great Britain, the United States, and throughout the world.

As we shall see, Joseph Lancaster was an empathetic young man who was profoundly moved by the plight of African slaves in the Caribbean. In a dramatic gesture during his early teens, he set out from his home in London to singlehandedly begin teaching the slaves to read.

Ultimately his adventure failed, and he was forced to return home. But his empathy for the unfortunate in society never ceased. Within just a few years he turned his attention to another group of individuals who needed his help. These were the children of a new class of working people in London, the industrial poor.

Industrial workers were relatively new in London society. They were not the proud artisans of the past whose work was respected by society and whose future appeared to be secure. These new laborers were the products of the machine age. Typically, they were unskilled and often toiled long hours for little pay. They had little status within society and their children had little hope for a stable future.

While many reform-minded individuals pitied their condition and despaired for their children, young Joseph Lancaster had a different perspective. For him, education was the answer. These children deserved a chance. And with the same determination he had to teach slaves, he set out to educate the children of the industrial poor.

He opened a small school in his father's home and began his ambitious enterprise. However, he soon outgrew this space and searched for larger accommodations. Joseph eventually found a warehouse, and with the generous support of his benefactors, he converted it into a suitable classroom.

When he opened his Boroughs Road School on January 1, 1798, Joseph Lancaster shook the world of education. But while he did have some support from both the Quaker church and as well as a number of reformers from the community, his financial position was always precarious.

Moreover, because his students could not afford to pay tuition, he was constantly searching for ways to keep his school open. He quickly learned to stretch his educational dollars and developed a variety of innovative methods to teach his students. Among these was the monitorial system. Here more advanced students taught younger students in small groups.

The success of the Boroughs Road School was dramatic. With his monitorial system he was able to teach upward of two to three hundred students at a time and did so on a shoestring budget. His methods caught the eye of reformers throughout Great Britain and eventually the United States, Mexico, and South America.

Lancaster traveled widely, gave lectures on his methods, and opened hundreds of schools throughout the world. Though his life was cut short when he was run over by an out-of-control carriage in New York City, his legacy lived on.

Not only had Lancaster established the importance of teaching poor children as well as the idea of free public education, his innovative methods of teaching, though sometimes controversial, sparked an important dialogue about the future of public education itself.

EMMA WILLARD—WOMEN'S EDUCATION

September 7, 1821

While the foundations of the common school movement were over a decade in the future and only a handful of women were receiving a formal education in the United States, Emma Willard shook the world of education on September 7, 1821, when she opened her Troy Female Seminary. This was the first school in the United States to offer both higher education and teacher training for women.

Her curriculum included such courses as mathematics, geography, philosophy, history, and science, but Emma also recognized the growing need for female teachers. In short, she pioneered equality of female education and teacher training education in the United States.

Emma Hart Willard was the sixteenth of seventeen children and grew up in a large farming family in Connecticut. Her father Samuel Hart was a Revolutionary War veteran and early social reformer who understood the importance of education for his children. Samuel held regular family discussions on the issues of the day, read aloud from the Bible and other books, and encouraged his children to read as well.

Emma's early education was at home. Her father recognized that she was a precocious child, and from an early age she sat on his lap as he read to her. As she matured, she read on her own and soon had consumed all the books in the household.

In 1802, at age fifteen Emma enrolled in her first school, a small academy in Worthington, Connecticut, about a mile from her home. Within just two years she became the teacher at the academy during the summer term! Two years later at the age of nineteen, she was placed in charge of the school and held that position during the winter term of 1806.

With this experience Emma was ready to begin her career as an educator. In the fall of 1807, she left home and was appointed principal of the prestigious Vermont Middlebury Female Seminary.

The two years at Middlebury, however, were a disappointment for Emma. The curriculum seemed tame, narrow, and lacked the academic rigor that she wanted. As a result, Emma left Middlebury, married a wealthy doctor, and began to raise her own family. Within just a few years, however, she returned to teaching and opened a boarding school for women in her own home.

Her school represented a break from the "finishing school" model of education for women at the time, in which sewing, flower arranging, polite manners, playing the piano, and singing were the primary educational objectives for women. While Emma was not opposed to preparing women for a life of middle-class motherhood, she felt strongly that they were equal to men intellectually and should have access to a rigorous course of study.

In June 1819, she began writing her seminal pamphlet *A Plan for Improving Female Education*. This work was widely read and gave her considerable renown. Bolstered by both encouragement and support, she presented her plan for a publicly funded female seminary to the members of the New York State Legislature.

While her plan was rejected out of hand by the conservative legislators who saw this kind of women's education as contrary to God's will, she persevered. Eventually she received funding from the city of Troy to open her Troy Female Seminary in September of 1821. Emma Willard forced open the doors of opportunity for women when she established her seminary and shook the world of education.

HORACE MANN—FATHER OF THE COMMON SCHOOL

June 29, 1837

Most educational reformers of this era focused their attention on the education of the rich and socially prominent. Joseph Lancaster, of course, desperately attempted to provide educational opportunities for the poor, and Emma Willard centered her attention on young women. But the broad American middle class, for the most part, had been ignored. It was this void that Horace Mann attempted to fill.

On a warm day in the summer of 1837, Mann shook the world of education by assuming the position of secretary of the Board of Education of Massachusetts and formally launching the common school movement in America.

Horace Mann embraced secular education as the key to successful schools. He saw free public education as the ideal and recognized the importance of state and municipal support of education. Above all, however, he embraced the idea of teaching children from all backgrounds and sought to establish a common learning experience to "equalize the conditions of men." He was a visionary.

Regarding teacher training, Mann rejected the monitorial system and argued that teachers needed intensive training in publicly funded "normal schools." Moreover, he argued that classrooms should be relatively small. These ideas, of course, challenged Lancaster's pragmatic approach of enormous classes taught by older, untrained students.

But like Lancaster, Horace Mann had little formal training in education. In fact, he had never set foot in a classroom as a teacher. Rather he was relatively unknown outside the state of Massachusetts when he was selected to head that state's new public school system as the secretary of the Board of Education.

Nevertheless, because of his remarkable work for twelve years in this position, today he is universally seen as the "father of the common school." One early educational historian, Ellwood Cubberley, captured the importance of Horace Mann for public education by noting that:

> no one did more than he to establish in the minds of the American people the conception that education should be universal, non-sectarian, free and that its aims should be social efficiency, civic virtue, and character, rather than mere learning.

As a committed social activist, Mann promoted important causes such as women's rights, temperance, adequate institutions for the insane, as well as the end of debtor's prison. But by directing his considerable efforts to the reform of education, he propelled the issue of the common school into the mainstream reform movement of this period. No longer a tangential concern, education now was a central part of the greater reform agenda.

One of the central turning points in Horace Mann's passionate embrace of reform came when he attended an oration by Ralph Waldo Emerson in 1837 titled "The American Scholar." In this seminal address, Emerson argued that "our day of dependence, our long apprenticeship to the learning of other lands draws to a close." It was time, he argued, that the United States stepped up and demanded its place in the world community.

Perhaps Emerson helped to inspire the younger Horace Mann of the importance of the common school when he went on to say, "I ask not for the great, the remote, the romantic . . . I embrace the common, I explore and sit at the feet of the familiar, the low."

Within days after attending this lecture, Horace Mann formally began his duties as secretary of the Board of Education in Massachusetts and launched the common school movement. His desire to teach all young men and women and to promote a common educational experience that emphasized civic virtue as well as the basics of learning introduced a new era in education that has been called the "greatest social experiment of man."

WILLIAM HOLMES MCGUFFEY — THE GRADED *READER*

April 1, 1836

As Horace Mann was launching the common school movement in 1837, the groundwork for a new, modern reading curriculum was being unveiled nearly nine hundred miles to the west at Miami College. This moment that shook the world of education came on April 1, 1836, when William McGuffey published the first *Reader*.

William Holmes McGuffey was teaching at Miami College in Oxford, Ohio, when he was contacted by the small publishing firm Truman and Smith to create and edit a series of readers for primary school students. Truman and Smith understood the need for a new set of readers that would essentially replace the age-old *New England Primer* that was sorely outdated by that time. Catherine Beecher Stowe, a friend of McGuffey, recommended him to the publishers, and he gladly accepted the assignment, receiving a substantial fee of $1,000.

What McGuffey created, however, was a sensation for educators and transformed the way that teachers taught and students learned. First, rather than simply presenting the material to be read with no introduction, McGuffey prefaced the reading lessons with his "Suggestions for Teachers."

His new vision of learning rejected simple memorization. He noted that "nothing can be more fatiguing to the teacher than a recitation conducted on . . . verbatim answers." Rather he suggested that teachers "try the *conversational* method of communicating instruction and training of the mind." He encouraged teachers to "use the questions, furnished in the book, as the basis of this method."

In short, rather than simply listening to students recite memorized material, teachers could more easily engage them through discussion that centered on questions from the readings. The shift from memorization to understanding had begun.

Second, by including discussion questions in his *Readers*, he opened the door to written examinations. Rather than simply assessing a student's progress by how well he or she recited memorized material or spelled words correctly in a spelling bee, teachers could determine whether a student understood the material that was being read.

And finally, and perhaps more important, the McGuffey *Readers* were "graded." As a new teacher at the age of fourteen, instructing a class of forty-five students on the Ohio frontier, McGuffey recognized that students were often confused and overwhelmed with the material presented to them. Excerpts from Shakespeare, Milton, or even the Bible were simply incomprehensible at a young age, though some could memorize a passage or two successfully.

As a result, McGuffey emphasized the importance of presenting material to students in a graded manner so they might understand what they were reading. This idea would later be the basis of the basal reader movement of the late nineteenth and early twentieth centuries. Here students progressed from one reading level to another once they had mastered and understood the material. With some important changes, this remains the primary approach to reading education today.

Old Guff, as McGuffey was affectionately called, was a modest and religious man who spent his entire life in the service of teaching. His *Readers*, however, transformed the small town professor into a national sensation. By the time of his death in 1872, his *Readers* had sold over fifty million copies, and today they are still in print and have sold over 120 million copies.

Though they seem quaint and a bit old fashioned today with their biblical imperatives and quotes from Revolutionary War heroes, this modest professor shook the world of education and placed it on a path toward the modern schools of today.

JOHN DEWEY—FATHER OF PROGRESSIVE EDUCATION

January 13, 1896

On January 13, 1896, John Dewey shook the world of education when he opened his famous laboratory school at the newly established University of Chicago. This school would transform our understanding of classroom teaching and helped to launch the modern progressive education movement.

While there were a number of progressive educators that would eventually contribute to the field, Dewey stood alone. Although many of his ideas were not embraced by the educational community during his early career, he is now seen as the crucial link between the work of scholars such as Pestalozzi and Rousseau and the neoprogressive reformers of the 1960s and beyond.

Like Pestalozzi, Dewey argued that learning could not take place in the abstract. Students must be able to connect the objects of a lesson with the ideas behind them. Moreover, like Rousseau, Dewey contended that student learning was most effective when they were interested in the subject matter.

For Dewey, however, the abstract nature of teaching that was so common in schools of that period reflected deeper problems for society. The rapid industrialization of the U.S. economy during the late nineteenth century had created a society that lacked an understanding of the interconnectedness of individuals.

Because of the rise of individualism associated with industrialization and the market economy, Dewey and other progressives maintained that we had become mere cogs in the machine, so specialized that we had lost our sense of community. Throughout his career as an educator and philosopher, Dewey argued that schools should not only promote the acquisition of basic knowledge but also should help reacquaint students with the basic interdependency of society.

In short, John Dewey like Horace Mann before him encouraged educators to expand the basic role of schools. Classrooms should not only promote knowledge and understanding but should also be places to help rebuild their communities. For Dewey, no man was an island despite America's growing embrace of individualism.

John Dewey's legacy for education was important not only for the early progressives but also for education today. His experiments with socially progressive classrooms in his lab school inspired a host of curricular innovations. These included inquiry-based instruction, individual contracting, preschool education, multi-age grouping, differential staffing, flexible scheduling, team teaching, and the open classroom.

The dialogue regarding the nature of teaching and learning was forever changed because of the ideas of this modest professor from Vermont.

W. E. B. DU BOIS—EQUALITY OF AFRICAN AMERICAN EDUCATION

January 1, 1903

W. E. B. Du Bois shook the world of education on January 1, 1903, when he challenged educational orthodoxy and demanded equal access to classical education for African Americans. While Emma Willard had opened the doors of higher education for women in the early nineteenth century, the struggle to achieve equal educational rights for African Americans was much longer and more protracted.

When African Americans eventually pushed their way into the schools of America, however, the perceived track for their education was vocational. Partly because of the need of black people to develop marketable skills in the growing industrial economy and partly because of a general stereotype of African Americans as intellectually inferior to white people, vocational education was seen as their proper direction.

By the end of the nineteenth century, several black colleges had been established with this vocational approach, initially with the assistance of black churches and later a handful of white philanthropic organizations. One of the most important of these black colleges was the Tuskegee Institute established by Booker T. Washington in 1881. Washington's vision for the institute was to promote vocational education for African Americans and provide them with marketable skills following graduation.

This approach attracted a great deal of attention, especially among white philanthropic organizations such as the Peabody, Slater, and Rosenwald groups. Eventually other wealthy individuals such as Andrew Carnegie and John D. Rockefeller would provide some support.

The success of Tuskegee and other similar institutions essentially confirmed the "logic" of a separate educational track for black people during this period with the implied idea that black people were incapable of a classical education. This notion, of course, appealed to many Americans (both Northerners and Southerners) during the Jim Crow era of the late nineteenth and early twentieth century.

But not all African Americans (and white people for that matter) supported Booker T. Washington's policies of accommodation or vocational education. Many were angered that he seemed to "look the other way" when it came to the injustices heaped upon black people during this era. And yet while others criticized Washington's ideas, W. E. B Du Bois was his most vocal critic. In 1903, Du Bois shook the world of education when he published *The Souls of Black Folk.*

In this important work, Du Bois criticized Washington for his silence regarding Jim Crow. Du Bois went on to call Washington "the most distinguished southerner since Jefferson Davis," the president of the Confederate States of America! But Du Bois saved his most searing criticism for Washington's vocational tracking idea. He recognized that African Americans needed marketable skills to survive in the racist world of Jim Crow, but he warned that the exclusive "tracking" of blacks into industrial occupations was dangerous and reinforced racial stereotypes.

Du Bois was a champion for equal educational opportunities for African Americans at a time when black people were struggling to achieve basic civil rights. His consistent support of classic education challenged what he called Washington's "gospel of work and money." In a later essay titled "The Talented Tenth" (referring to the educated elite of the African American community), Du Bois articulated an essential principle of education not only for African Americans but for all Americans. He wrote,

> If we make money the object of [education], we shall develop money-makers but not necessarily men. . . . [I]ntelligence, broad sympathy, knowledge of the world that was and is, and of the relation of men to it—this is the curriculum . . . which must underlie true life.

Du Bois clearly shook the world of education and opened the door to a new generation of African American educators who would challenge the inherent biases in our educational system.

HORACE MANN BOND – A CHALLENGE TO STANDARDIZED TESTING

March 1, 1924

One such challenge came from Horace Mann Bond who on March 1, 1924, shook the world of education by rejecting the fundamental basis of standardized exams and IQ testing in America. Bond argued that the cultural biases inherent in these tests had unfairly labeled African Americans as intellectually inferior.

For over a quarter of a century, the standardized testing movement had been growing dramatically. Led by such legendary figures as Sir Francis Galton who had spent his career studying human differences, the world had become fascinated with the idea that we could accurately measure intelligence with a simple test.

In 1903, Alfred Binet had developed a multiple choice prototype of the standardized test in France to identify learning disabled children. In his book *Studies in Intelligence* published that same year, Binet created an instrument that could distinguish between "the normal child and the abnormal."

Two years later Binet and his student Theodore Simon introduced an improved examination that they called the Binet Simon scale (later known as the Stanford Binet test). This became the standard of intelligence testing for the next half century.

The work of Binet, Simon, and others during this period created tests as diagnostic instruments to identify students with learning problems. But a darker side of testing also was emerging at this time—one designed to sort individuals based on race and ethnicity.

In his *Inquiries into Human Faculty and Its Development* published in 1908 and then his article titled "Essays in Eugenics" published the following year, Galton gave credence to the dangerous idea of the innate superiority of the "white race."

Concerned with the perceived decline of intelligence in Great Britain at this time, he recommended early marriage of "promising" upper-class couples who would be subsidized to produce large families and thus enhance the intelligence of his homeland.

In the United States, G. Stanley Hall, president of Clark University and founder of the *Journal of Psychology*, had similar recommendations. He called for selective breeding and even forced sterilization of the "defective, the weak and the sick."

The diagnostic and sorting approaches to testing were evident in 1917 when the United States entered World War I. During this difficult period, it embarked on the most expansive testing program ever attempted. Between 1917 and November 1918 when the war ended, the United States had tested nearly two million "doughboys" using the so-called Alpha and Beta tests.

And although these tests were flawed in many ways, their apparent success, the overall support given to them by the U.S. Army, and the Allied victory over Germany and the Central Powers fueled the testing movement.

Within months following the end of the war, tests were being developed for schools across the nation, and the unquestioning acceptance of the validity of the exams themselves had given the eugenics movement incredible momentum.

One of the key players in the development and application of the Alpha and Beta tests was Carl Brigham. He statistically analyzed the overall results of the tests and in 1923 published a massive volume titled *A Study of American Intelligence*.

In this book Brigham proclaimed the intellectual superiority of the Nordic race and the inferiority of "Mediterranean" and "Negro" races. He went on to say that there was no doubt that American Negros, Italians, and Jews were "genetically ineducable." It was a waste of money, he continued, "to try to give those born morons and imbeciles a good Anglo-Saxon education."

Reinforcing prevailing racist attitudes of the day, many Americans accepted Brigham's interpretation and assumed that they were based on science and logic. The 1920s, after all, had witnessed a dramatic upsurge in membership of the Ku Klux Klan throughout the nation as well as passage of restrictive immigration legislation known as the National Origins Acts.

But it was a young Horace Mann Bond who vigorously challenged the efficacy of these results. As a historian, educator, and early civil rights activist, Bond demonstrated the fundamental misinterpretation of testing data as well as the inherent cultural bias of the tests themselves.

Bond continued to challenge the value of these exams and the inaccurate misinterpretations of findings based on these exams. As late as 1958, he rebuked a study of the inferior intelligence of black people by Audrey Shuey, noting that all she had proven was that "everywhere in the United States the American Negro is a subordinated underprivileged social caste."

While he was unable to check the growing acceptance of standardized tests in the United States along with the racial stereotyping that came with it, Bond shook the world of education in March 1924 when he offered the first major challenge to the idea of standardized testing in schools.

THURGOOD MARSHALL—THE END OF LEGAL SEGREGATION

May 17, 1954

On May 17, 1954, Thurgood Marshall shook the world of education when he successfully argued the *Brown v. Board of Education* case before the U.S. Supreme Court and signaled the end of legal segregation in American public schools. Thurgood Marshall, of course, was not alone in this struggle. He represented a long line of reformers and activists who had fought for equal rights of African Americans and who challenged racial stereotypes and centuries of blatant racism.

While the common school had symbolically promised an education for all, one group of Americans was systematically excluded: African slaves. With few exceptions, slaves had no access to education and were certainly not part of the great common school movement in the three decades preceding the American Civil War.

In fact, following the Denmark Vesey slave revolt of 1822 and the Nat Turner rebellion less than a decade later, states throughout the South passed legislation that made it a crime to teach slaves and for slaves to be taught. It was considered too dangerous for African Americans to receive an education. In some southern states, slaves caught learning to read were subject to "39 lashes on his or her bare back."

These egregious legal restrictions ended with the conclusion of the Civil War, but the struggle for equal education continued through Reconstruction, Jim Crow, and well into the twentieth century.

For a moment following the Civil War, however, freed slaves (called freedmen) had a chance at education with the creation of the Freedmen's Bureau Schools in 1865. These schools taught young black boys and girls as well as older former slaves. In addition, thousands of poor white people also attended these schools.

At its peak in 1869 the Freedmen's Bureau had recruited over nine thousand teachers. When the program ended in the early 1870s, over four thousand schools had been established and nearly a quarter million students had received a basic education.

But soon Jim Crow descended on America and support for African American education all but disappeared. Then in 1896, the famous *Plessy v. Ferguson* Supreme Court decision gave a false legitimacy to segregation with its "separate but equal" ruling. This decision would stall progress toward African American education for over a half-century.

Early civil rights activists such as W. E. B Du Bois fought for equal access to classical education and helped establish the NAACP in 1909. It was this organization under the direction of figures such as Charles Hamilton

Houston and later Du Bois that challenged Jim Crow discrimination laws through the courts.

Houston, a U.S. Army veteran in World War I who served with distinction in France, returned from the war determined to challenge the sort of "hate and scorn showered on . . . Negros by our fellow Americans." He was determined to work through America's legal system. Houston once stated, "I made up my mind that if I got through this war, I would study law and use my time fighting for men who could not strike back."

His storied career included becoming dean of Howard School of Law and the first special consul of the NAACP. Moreover, with his students, including Thurgood Marshall, he challenged residential covenant laws (that excluded black people) as well as disenfranchisement laws, common throughout the South during this period.

Working with Marshall (who argued the case before the Supreme Court), Houston took on the mighty Democratic Party of Texas that had used a 1923 law to exclude black people from voting in primaries in that state.

Arguing successfully that the Fourteenth and Fifteenth Amendments to the Constitution had forbidden voting discrimination based on race, the *Smith v. Allwright* decision of 1944 set the stage for expanded voting rights for black people and other minorities and provided a legal argument to effectively challenge the "separate but equal" concept of *Plessy v. Ferguson*.

The defining moment of change that shook the world of education, however, came on May 17, 1954, when the Supreme Court declared, in a unanimous decision, that segregated schools were unconstitutional. Although schools, especially in the South, were often slow to desegregate, the doors of educational opportunity for African Americans and other minorities had now opened slightly.

THE KIDS ARE ALL RIGHT—POLITICAL ACTIVISM

February 14, 2018

On a sunny Valentine's Day afternoon, February 14, 2018, a former student from Marjory Stoneman Douglas High School in Parkland, Florida, entered the school and opened fire with his AR-15 semiautomatic rifle. Within just minutes, seventeen young high school students lay dead in the halls and classrooms of this upscale suburban school.

After hundreds of students screamed and ran for their lives, a small group of young men and women angrily demanded immediate changes in our federal gun safety laws and protection of American schools.

Among those defiant students from Marjory Stoneman Douglas High School that day was senior David Hogg. His simple message to the American people was "enough is enough!" The carnage of nearly twenty years of school shootings beginning in 1999 at Columbine High School through the slaughter of huddled, crying first and second graders in Newtown, Connecticut, and now the mass killing of seventeen students at his school was simply too much.

Hogg and other Parkland kids shook the world of education on that day as they demanded immediate action of school safety. Defiantly challenging the hollow "thoughts and prayers" mantra emanating from local, state, and national leaders, they called upon their fellow students to spread the message of #neveragain.

The actions of David Hogg, Emma Gonzalez, Cameron Kasky, and others led to the organization of an unprecedented March for Our Lives: Road to Change Tour in sixty-eight cities in the summer of 2018 and has empowered students throughout the country to force politicians to address the issue of school safety.

While school safety is one of the central issues facing education today, what is remarkable is that this movement is student powered through social media and public demonstration. This represents a new student-centered approach to demand changes in school policy.

Throughout our educational history there have been numerous cases of students (and parents) vigorously challenging school policy. Typically, however, these were spontaneous actions at the local level or through the courts.

In early nineteenth-century New York, for example, a group of students acted against a particularly violent teacher after he injured a small boy with his ferule. The older boys picked him up, carried him out of the school, and pushed him down an icy hill. The teacher in question, Mr. Augusta Starr, "looked up at the mutinous crew [mumbled incoherently] . . . and was never seen again."

Another example of grassroots student protests against school policy was when a group of students and their parents from Chicago protested the suspension of a popular teacher by the new centralized school administration. The students staged a walkout of Andrew Jackson School in the spring of 1900 and marched to the home of a local alderman—the notorious Johnny Powers—to get relief, and the teacher was reinstated.

Then, beginning in the late 1960s through the next decade, students routinely challenged the school policy of *in loco parentis* and demanded individual student rights. In a series of legal disputes, student and their parents secured the rights of parental access to personal records, a measure of freedom of speech and the right to due process when accused of a crime or rule infraction.

In short, there has been a long history of student and parental challenges to the policies of schools. But the situation in Parkland was different. Here students went beyond their teachers, principals, administrators, and often parents and took to the streets to challenge local, state, and national leaders to act immediately on school safety.

The actions of the Parkland kids led by David Hogg, Emma Gonzalez, Cameron Kasky, and others shook the world of education. By giving voice to students themselves with social media and "old school" demonstrations, they have moved the critical issue of gun safety to the center of our political discourse.

From the writings of Jean-Jacques Rousseau; the early schools for the poor of Joseph Lancaster; through the challenges to educational policy by W. E. B. Du Bois, John Dewey, and Horace Mann Bond; to the demands for gun safety legislation by David Hogg, Emma Gonzalez, Cameron Kasky, and others, there were a number of critical moments that shook the world of education.

By understanding the importance of these *Ten Days That Shook the World of Education*, we can better appreciate the critical role that everyday people have played by standing up against injustice and challenging educational policy.

Chapter One

Jean-Jacques Rousseau—The Philosophy of Modern Education

Spring 1762

It was the spring of 1762. France was twenty-five years from its revolution in 1787 and the North American colonies, fresh from the Seven Years' War with France and her Native American allies, were still fourteen years from their revolution in 1776.

And yet during April and May of 1762 Jean-Jacques Rousseau shook the world of education. That spring the influential scholar, reformer, and activist penned two books that would alter the course of educational thought for generations to come.

TWO SEMINAL WORKS

These two books were very different. The first, *The Social Contract*, published in April of 1762, was an important philosophical tract that influenced generations of reformers from Thomas Paine and Karl Marx to Johann Wolfgang von Goethe and Leo Tolstoy. The ideas presented in this book, moreover, were the foundation stones for both the American and French Revolutions.

Rousseau's novel, *Emile, or On Education*, on the other hand, was equally as influential and impacted generations of educational reformers such as Maria Montessori, Jacques Derrida, and John Dewey, to name just a few.

Figure 1.1. Jean-Jacques Rousseau. Source: Painted portrait by unknown artist, circa late 1700s.

CRITICISM BY CHURCH AND STATE

And yet despite their importance, both books were banned in France and Switzerland. Because of Rousseau's rejection of both original sin and divine revelation, he angered Protestant and Roman Catholic authorities alike. In fact, the Archbishop of Paris once condemned him *by name* from the pulpit, and soon his books were being burned in the streets.

The French Parliament also was outraged by Rousseau's *Emile* and issued a warrant for his arrest. As a result, he was forced to flee the country and return to Geneva. Here too he received a cool reception and his books were widely condemned.

RECOGNITION FROM ENLIGHTENMENT FIGURES

On the other hand, Voltaire, David Hume, and many other Enlightenment philosophers celebrated Rousseau's philosophical ideas, especially his position on religion. Voltaire actually invited Rousseau to live with him, writing, "Let him come here to [my estate]. He must come! I shall receive him with open arms . . . and treat him like my own son." Rousseau never took up Voltaire's kind offer, but later he wrote that he regretted not doing so.

Then in July 1762, just months after the publication of his two masterpieces, he was expelled from his boyhood home of Bern, Switzerland.

FUGITIVE AND EXILE

Eventually he made his way to Motiers, Switzerland, where he lived as a fugitive for several years. Once again he angered church officials who demanded that he formally answer charges of blasphemy! Rousseau was courteous but replied that he could not come to answer these charges because he had difficulty sitting for long periods of time. Church officials were not amused.

When his local pastor denounced him publicly and referred to him as the antichrist, Rousseau endured a very difficult period. He was stoned in public places and his home was vandalized. Once again it was time for Rousseau to leave town. He relocated to the small island of Ile de St. Pierre—but here too he was not welcome.

CHANGING FORTUNES

Rousseau's fortunes changed abruptly, however, when he finally secured a passport to Paris. In December 1765 he reentered the city of lights and took up residence at the palace of a friend, the Prince of Conti. Rousseau had now become a celebrity. David Hume, the great historian and Enlightenment figure, wrote, "No person ever so much enjoyed . . . such attention. . . . Voltaire and everybody else are quite eclipsed."

Thus in the three years from the publication of *The Social Contract* and *Emile*, Rousseau had endured criticism and censure, was forced to leave two countries, was called out for blasphemy, was stoned as he walked in public places, and had his house vandalized.

Rousseau's newfound celebrity was due partly to the persecution he had endured from the church, but it was also because of the dramatic effect these two works had on the intellectual community.

THE SOCIAL CONTRACT

The primary focus of *The Social Contract* was the difficulty of establishing a sense of community in a world that had become commercialized. The problem as Rousseau saw it was that as humankind evolved from a state of nature to a modern society, individuals had gradually lost their freedom and innocence.

As the state grew and its attendant bureaucracy expanded, the freedom of the people suffered. The solution, he argued, was to maintain smaller city-states that were too weak to exert undue power over the people.

But embedded within Rousseau's political/philosophical tract was a powerful principle for the future of education. This idea was the inherent goodness of man. Individuals, he argued, were not born wicked or evil because of original sin as argued by the church but rather were pure at birth. It was our modern political society that corrupted man.

THE ESSENTIAL GOODNESS OF MAN

For Rousseau, "man is born free but everywhere he is in chains." This idea would become central to educational reform. If children were born pure and free, then routine severe discipline, typical in the schools of that time, was not only unnecessary but also dangerous—in fact, it helped to corrupt them.

Similarly, Rousseau tacitly rejected the powerful ideas of John Locke, who had argued that a child was born as a blank slate—a tabula rasa—and therefore education was metaphorically perceived as simply filling an empty vessel.

ADDRESSING JOHN LOCKE'S IDEAS

Though Locke's work was an important step in rejecting the biblical concept of the inherent depravity of man, Rousseau went further. He argued that children were not depraved, nor were they blank slates. Rather they possessed an inherent sense of freedom and goodness. As a result, education should draw on the interests and ideas of students to achieve educational results.

THE CHILD-CENTERED APPROACH TO EDUCATION

These simple concepts had a profound impact on educators. The essential components of a "child-centered" approach to education were now in place. In addition to rejecting the Judeo-Christian notion that children were stained at birth with the original sin, Rousseau also challenged some of the basic principles of Christian teaching.

A CHALLENGE TO THE CHURCH: SECULAR EDUCATION

Perhaps the most important of these, for education, was his characterization of the church. Rousseau argued that there were three kinds of religions: the religion of man, the religion of the citizen, and "a strange third kind" that he referred to as the religion of the priest.

The religion of man had "no temple, no altar, no ritual" and consisted of what he called "internal worship." The religion of the citizen, on the other hand, was the religion of a specific country and had "its dogmas, its rights, its visible forms of worship, ordained by law." Finally, the "strange" third kind of religion was like the Christianity of Rome in which there was a dual authority of both the priest and secular leaders.

For Rousseau, it was the "religion of man" that was the best. It had no formal structure but simply allowed salvation directly between God and man. The second type of formalized religion was flawed in that it regarded those individuals who were not part of the congregation as "faithless, alien and barbarian." This was dangerous for society. The "strange religion" of dual authority Rousseau rejected outright. He wrote that it "was so obviously bad that it was a waste of time bothering to prove it."

CRITICISM BY PROTESTANTS AND CATHOLICS

As might be expected, Rousseau was criticized by both Protestants and Roman Catholics for these views, and, as we have seen, it led to his exile from both France and Switzerland. And yet Rousseau was a spiritual man and though he was attracted to the idea of Deism he remained a Roman Catholic throughout much of his life after he renounced his boyhood Calvinism.

Nevertheless, while Rousseau's *The Social Contract* was widely criticized by the church, his fundamental idea of the goodness of man as well as his embrace of secular education would become the centerpiece of educational reform for the next two centuries.

EMILE

Rousseau's second masterwork of 1762, the novel *Emile*, further developed the general concept of the child-centered approach to education. Through his description of the life of Emile from his early life through maturity and adulthood, Rousseau not only gave readers a sense of the "stages of development" of the child but also helped educators understand the best methods of teaching children at each of these important stages.

AGE OF NATURE

During the "Age of Nature," from infancy through about age five, for example, learning was achieved in a free and open environment. Tutors should not "teach" as such but simply guide the child through various experiences and protect him or her from harm.

Children at this stage of learning should be as free as possible and not constrained or confined because of their behavior or the customs of the community. Rousseau wrote that infants were like "small animals" and should be free from restrictive swaddling clothes. In the next few years they should be free to explore their own interests and creatively imagine solutions to their own childish dilemmas.

Rousseau also recommended that infants be breastfed by their own mothers and not a wet nurse, as was the custom of the day among the wealthy. Once they were old enough, they should be allowed to play outside in nature as much as possible. Rousseau argued that this approach to education would allow them to develop their physical senses, that they would use throughout their lives.

EDUCATION FOR CHILDHOOD

In the second stage of education, what Rousseau called "Education for Childhood" or the period of "sense education," students would continue to develop their reasoning power. However, this learning should come from within. The tutor should not "instruct" students but instead provide moral training through example.

In addition, Rousseau introduced the "theory of natural consequences" as part of this stage of development. Here students would learn, through their own experiences, what they can and cannot do. Tutors should allow students to make mistakes or even "act out." But then those students must live with the consequences of their own actions.

For example, if a child breaks a toy in anger, he or she should not be punished as such, but the toy would not be replaced. The tutor or teacher would then explain that this was the consequence of the child's own actions.

ROUSSEAU'S PERMISSIVENESS IS CRITICIZED

This "permissiveness" was of course challenged by church leaders and traditional educators alike. Churchmen argued that by allowing this sort of freedom, children would be introduced to evil. Secular educators, on the other hand, saw this approach as a waste of precious time for the intellectual development of the child.

Nevertheless, Rousseau defended his position by arguing that children under the age of twelve were essentially incapable of traditional learning and needed to develop their imagination, experiences, ideas, and physical sense to have a context upon which future learning could be based.

AGE OF SOCIAL REASONING

It was in the next stage of development, what Rousseau referred to as the "Age of Social Reasoning," that students would begin their "formal" education. Beginning at about age twelve, they would embark on a two-pronged approach to education.

The first was vocational. Rousseau believed strongly that every man should have a marketable skill that could be used in case of misfortune. This might include an economic collapse, a social upheaval, or a personal tragedy.

THE IMPORTANCE OF LEARNING A TRADE

Additionally, by learning a trade such as carpentry, students would develop physical abilities, motor skills, and "hand-brain coordination." These physical skills would be essential as they progressed to more intellectual pursuits and the acquisition of knowledge.

This idea certainly came from Rousseau's personal experience as a child. When he was a young boy, Rousseau's father lost his business as a wine merchant. As a result, the Rousseaus were forced to sell the family estate and move to an artisan neighborhood. It was there that his father took up a trade as a watchmaker.

This memory was seared into Rousseau's consciousness and he recognized the importance of having a skill that would help keep him and his family from poverty.

AN ACADEMIC EDUCATION BEGINS

Once a student had been introduced to skills in a trade, he or she was ready to move to more intellectual pursuits. But even here, he or she should not be coerced into learning. Rousseau argued that only when a student "desired to learn" could effective learning take place.

For example, as Emile began to mature, he received several party invitations addressed to him. He tried to have someone in the household read these invitations to him, but everyone refused. As a result, Emile "needed" and wanted to learn to read—and so he did.

THE IMPORTANCE OF EXPERIENCE

As Emile developed his reading skills, he was gradually introduced to subjects such as astronomy, geography, and science. Learning, however, was not centered on textbooks that Rousseau saw as having little importance. Rather knowledge should be acquired through experiences in nature.

For example, Emile was introduced to astronomy by the tutor. He took him to see the sunrise in the middle of the summer (near the summer solstice) and then brought him to the same place around Christmas (the winter solstice) to demonstrate the movement of the earth around the sun and how the tilting of the earth in the northern hemisphere affected seasonal changes.

Another example is when Emile resisted the study of geography, especially the idea of using the sun for directions. The tutor then took Emile on a walk in the woods. Emile was excited and had fun with his tutor. Then suddenly they found themselves lost. It was hot and both were getting hungry.

They sat down on a log to rest and Emile started to cry. The tutor then consoled Emile and began to reflect on what they had learned earlier about the movement of the sun and how it affected the shadows of trees.

By reasoning, Emile began to understand that because his home was to the south, he could use the shadows to guide his way. The two followed a path to the south and soon arrived back at home—safe and sound. These ideas were the genesis of the seminal educational principle of John Dewey "learning by doing" that had a dramatic impact on the development of progressive education beginning in the twentieth century.

ROBINSON CRUSOE

The only book that Rousseau recommended during this period of development was Daniel Defoe's *Robinson Crusoe* (not the Bible). Here Rousseau noted that Robinson's self-reliance and ingenuity allowed him to survive on an uninhabited island. These were important ideas for students to learn.

Rousseau wrote that this one book was Emile's entire library for several years and served as the basis of discussions on the natural sciences. When Emile was puzzled by a problem in science, he and the tutor would discuss how Robinson addressed the problem. (WWRD!)

By linking firsthand experiences and observations of nature with this novel about self-reliance and ingenuity, Emile learned. Here was the basis of his education during this stage of development.

RELIGION: THE VICAR OF SAVOYARD

During this period, Emile also was introduced to religion through the Vicar of Savoyard, his spiritual mentor. The vicar was a humble village priest, but he had many experiences and possessed an intuitive sense of morality. He taught Emile a great deal about the place of religion in his life.

Among the most important ideas of the Vicar was what has been called indifferentism—the notion that all religions were essentially alike and that one should follow the religion best suited to oneself. He also noted that God and religion should be revealed freely by the individual and not forced upon the child. In short, the Vicar urged Emile to be skeptical about religion and use his inner moral compass to help him select the proper faith.

SELECTING A PROPER FAITH

Though not directly addressing the issue of secular education as he did in the *Social Contract*, Rousseau argued that the contradictory elements of formalized religion could confuse students and make it difficult for young men to understand their role in society and their place in the social contract.

Rousseau used the character of the Vicar to illustrate these ideas. The Vicar understood that different visions of the world by both philosophers and religious leaders could be confusing. His solution was to embrace knowledge that directly affected him and was meaningful to his life and to "leave all the rest in uncertainty without rejecting or accepting it and without tormenting himself to clarify it if it leads to nothing useful for practice."

AGE OF WISDOM

Once Emile received training in a trade, had mastered his basic subjects, and had been introduced to religion through the Vicar of Savoyard, he reached what Rousseau called the "Age of Wisdom." It was during this period that Emile entered society and, because of his education and experiences, would not be corrupted by it.

During this period, Emile's "isolation" ended, and he began to take an interest in others. Nevertheless, he was cautioned about the dangers facing him at this stage. The most important of these was the possibility of developing an *amour-propre* or self-love.

TWO FORMS OF "SELF-LOVE"

This form of self-love was based on the esteem derived from others. Rousseau argued that this represented a central element of our corrupt modern society that could cause misery for the individual.

Rather, throughout his life, Emile had been encouraged to develop a different form of self-love, what Rousseau called *amour de soi*. This form of self-love, he argued, was a more primitive instinct and emanated from the superior natural state of man. Emile had been taught to be proud of himself, to be self-confident and self-reliant. These characteristics developed through his education and experiences represent a self-love that looked inward and not to the praise, adoration, and approval of others in society.

SOPHIE

During this stage of development, Emile also met Sophie and experienced love for the first time. For Rousseau this was a natural and important part of his development. Eventually Emile and Sophie would get married and begin a family.

Rousseau saw Sophie as the perfect mate for Emile. She had a modest education that was "appropriate" for a woman at the time. This included some intellectual development so that she could read and keep the accounts of the household. But she must also be able to sing, play the harpsichord, and keep house. Sophie met these basic criteria but she also was skilled in dressmaking, sewing, and lacemaking.

ROUSSEAU IS CRITICIZED FOR HIS POSITION REGARDING WOMEN

Unlike Emile, who had the benefit of a tutor, Sophie had no formal education. Her mother had attended to her training from an early age and had prepared her for married, domestic life. Sophie was encouraged to become a moral woman, tend to the needs and entertainment of her husband and guests, and raise healthy, well-balanced children.

Rousseau wrote that "in the union of the sexes" each contributes to their common aim but not in the same way. The man ought to be active and strong while the woman passive and weak. One is dominant while the other does not resist.

As expected, Rousseau was criticized for his position on the role of women in society by early feminists such as Mary Wollstonecraft. She and others argued that Rousseau had sought to confine women to the household rather than recognize their abilities outside the domestic sphere.

PLACING ROUSSEAU IN HISTORICAL CONTEXT

While this argument certainly resonates with us today, Rousseau must also be understood in the context of the period. He did recognize women as equal but different. Both men and women, he wrote, had a role to play within the household that was central to the maintenance of a happy life.

Sophie, like all women, was equal to man in the sense that "each in fulfilling nature's ends according to its own particular purpose were thereby less perfect than if it resembled the other more!" In short men and women were "equal" in what they have in common but not comparable in ways they differed.

Thus concludes the education of Emile. Although we may want more, we must be content, at this point, to understand his early instruction and the principles set forth by Rousseau though this important novel. Did Emile have a happy life? Did his education provide him with the knowledge, experiences, and moral training that would guide him well? The answer is probably yes, though further study of the novel is necessary to develop an informed decision.

UNDERSTANDING ROUSSEAU'S WORLD

Once again, we must keep in mind that Rousseau penned this novel in 1762, and though many of his ideas seem fresh today, others do not. Certainly his perspective on women is outdated, leading many contemporary scholars to criticize him as an enemy of feminism. Similarly, the education of Emile was that of a gentleman and not the common folk of the period.

But Rousseau must be understood in the context of his period: the Enlightenment. The philosophers of this era—including Rousseau—were situated in a sort of transitional state. They struggled to resolve the exciting discoveries of the Scientific Revolution, on the one hand, and the firm grip that the church continued to maintain on the people.

ROUSSEAU AS A MAN OF THE ENLIGHTENMENT

Rousseau, as we have seen, was a devout Christian and a member of the Roman Catholic Church for much of his adult life. Nevertheless, he was attracted to Deism in that he embraced a supreme spiritual entity but was critical of formalized religion.

It is through this lens that we must understand Rousseau. He embraced a more modern vision of women's role in society and saw them as equal to men in some ways.

CONFLICTING VISIONS OF WOMEN

In *The Social Contract*, for example, he wrote that women must be included in what he called the "sovereign" component of political society. This element represented the "general will" of the population of which women were an important part.

On the other hand, Rousseau's description of Sophie in *Emile* suggests that he saw women primarily as "helpmates" who should submit to their husbands, manage the household for him and the children, and provide entertainment for the family and guests. There was no role for Sophie outside the domestic sphere.

EDUCATION OF ELITE GENTLEMEN

Regarding Rousseau's perspective on education we must again understand the period in which he lived. Education during the eighteenth century and into the nineteenth was the province of men from the wealthy middle class and the nobility.

And of course there were no public schools. Education for the poor, artisans, and farmers was relegated to apprenticeship to a trade or learning the skills of farming from fathers and grandfathers. Formal education with a tutor was reserved for the wealthy and the emerging class of professionals and proprietors. Emile, the gentleman, received this form of education.

LEGACY

Nevertheless, Rousseau shook the world of education to its core in the spring of 1762 with the publication of *The Social Contract* and *Emile*. These two works would help shape the world of education for the next two centuries.

His idea that individuals enter the world free and pure only to be corrupted by the absurdities of modern society changed the way we view children and how they learn. Children were not depraved, nor were they empty vessels as John Locke had argued a half century before. Rather they had an innate sense of goodness, morality, and curiosity. Therefore learning could take place by building on these values.

Moreover, because children did not enter this world as wicked or evil, as the church had taught for over a millennium, severe discipline was not only unnecessary but counterproductive. Other forms of discipline were now demanded given this new perspective.

Rousseau also embraced the concept of secular education, and because of his gravitas this idea became more acceptable to the general population. He essentially argued that in a society in which there was dual authority of church and state, a confusing conflict of ideas would develop.

The conflict between the laws of the church and the secular laws of society made it difficult for students to develop properly. Secular education separated from the realm of the church was the proper environment for education.

It was these important ideas that shook the world of education in the spring of 1762 and moved us toward a more child-centered vision of education. The world of education would never be the same.

Chapter Two

Joseph Lancaster—Teaching the Poor

January 1, 1798

As the world prepared to move into the nineteenth century, change was in the air. New religions were revolutionizing our philosophies, democracy was slowly remaking our political world, and the Industrial Revolution was transforming our economy and society.

Then on January 1, 1798, Joseph Lancaster shook the world of education when he opened his Borough Road School with over three hundred students. It was this day in educational history that the ideas of universal education, teaching the poor, and the model of the modern public school became a reality.

TEACHING THE POOR

At a time when public education, much less universal education, was virtually unknown, Joseph Lancaster was among the first to recognize the need to teach the poor. Joseph was an empathetic young man, and at the age of fourteen years he was so moved when he read an article on slavery that he set out for Jamaica to teach. Though he never reached the West Indies, his determination to help provide an education for the disadvantaged never wavered.

LANCASTER'S FIRST SCHOOL

At the age of fifteen, Lancaster joined the Society of Friends and began his teaching career in a Quaker school. He opened his first school in 1796 in his

Figure 2.1. Joseph Lancaster. Source: Portrait by unknown artist, circa 1860.

father's home on Kent Street in Southwark. Later he would write that "the undertaking [his first school] was begun under the roof of an affectionate parent [who] gave the schoolroom rent free, and, after fitting up the desks and forms myself [I enrolled] ninety children under my instruction."

Lancaster's reputation grew rapidly, as did the number of students he taught. He soon outgrew the Kent Street location and sought a larger school in London. With the help of several Quaker philanthropists, he secured a large warehouse in 1797, fitted it with desks and other classroom basics, and made plans for his new school. On New Year's Day 1798, Lancaster's dream became a reality and the world of education was changed forever.

A NEW CLASS OF POOR

Like many others of his generation, Lancaster was appalled at the growing number of extremely poor children in his community of Southwark, just outside London. The Industrial Revolution had spawned a new generation of young, uneducated boys and girls whose parents worked in factories and sweatshops.

But unlike many other reformers, Lancaster acted. He was determined to provide an education to these children whose future was bleak indeed. He recruited his students from the streets of Southwark and London and single-handedly launched the seminal idea of universal education.

THE BOROUGH ROAD SCHOOL

It is important to remember that when the Borough Road School opened, most British and American children had no access to education. So-called public schools did exist in England, but they were far from "public." In fact, these institutions were private schools that catered to the children of the nobility and the wealthy upper middle class of merchants, proprietors, and professionals. In short, you needed both the "proper" background and the tuition in order to attend.

In the United States, the Puritans of New England had embraced a form of public education beginning in the 1630s. And though well intentioned, these schools were limited to young Puritan children. Those with different religions need not apply.

And of course some educators over the years had sought to teach both slaves and the very poor. These efforts, however, were limited to the work of single individuals and often were short lived. Thus both the idea and the implementation of universal public education was little more than a dream of reformed-minded educators.

Joseph Lancaster emerged from rather ordinary circumstances but achieved great success in the field of education. Armed only with his great sense of empathy and a desire to help change the world through education, he faced off against the forces of industrialization and the powerful Market Revolution.

A MARKET-BASED PEDAGOGY

Lancaster understood well that while the emerging free market economy had created enormous wealth and power for some, it also had spawned a new generation of uneducated young men and women who had little hope for the future.

But rather than challenging the Market Revolution, he embraced many of its concepts and incorporated them into his schools. This new economy was the most powerful revolutionary force of the eighteenth and nineteenth centuries. It not only restructured our economic and political systems, it also redefined social relationships and, as we will see, helped visionaries like Lancaster to create a new school pedagogy that was in many ways a reflection of the dramatic changes ahead.

Some scholars have noted that Lancaster created a market-based pedagogy that promoted a model of the modern school and classroom. David Hogan, for example, has argued that the Lancaster system was based on "individual, competition, a meritocratic structure [and] a classroom psychology [of] scarcity, desire, ambition, shame and habituation."

THE LINK BETWEEN TRADITIONAL AND MODERN EDUCATION

In short, Lancaster's classrooms were a microcosm of the emerging competitive world of this new economy. And unlike most schools at this time, the "controlling concepts and metaphors [of Lancaster's schools] were commercial and disciplinary, not religious," despite the fact that he was a deeply religious man. Clearly Lancaster was a critical link between older forms of religious-based training and secular/nonsectarian education.

A MODEL FOR MODERN SCHOOLS

In addition to his important work in promoting the idea of universal education, Lancaster also created a model for schools today. Elements of this model included a nonsecular approach to education, public funding of schools, the placement of students in "classes" according to their ability, simultaneous instruction, competitive examinations complete with incentives for excellence, and a disciplinary system based on rewards and mild humiliation rather than corporal punishment.

NONSECTARIAN EDUCATION

Although Lancaster was a convert to the Society of Friends (Quakers), he insisted that his schools remain nonsectarian. He recognized early on that his students came from all walks of life and embraced a variety of religious beliefs and cultures. Rather than demanding adherence to a faith, he promoted Christian morality in a nonsectarian context.

This idea was a distinct shift from most schools at this time that were centered on religious education. As we have seen, for example, the schools of New England, often admired as the first public schools in the nation, clearly focused on the ideas and religious values of Calvinism.

THE *NEW ENGLAND PRIMER*

The famed *New England Primer* provided the core of those values. In fact, the term *primer* originally referred to a book of prayers and devotions and included the Lord's Prayer, the Ten Commandments, and a selection of scriptures.

The *Primer* used in these and other schools of the period typically reduced biblical teachings to simple axioms that could be memorized and then recited by children. Thus we read, "In Adam's fall, we sinned all" or "Whales in the sea, God's voice obey," or "Zaccheus did climb the tree, His Lord to see."

A PAN PROTESTANT APPROACH TO EDUCATION

While these ideas were important to Lancaster, he did not impose them on his students. Rather he promoted a kind of "pan-Protestantism" in the classroom. This approach eventually became the centerpiece of instruction in the common schools of the United States during the nineteenth century.

By then most educators accepted this important point. D. P. Page, the great pedagogue, for example, wrote, "We are dependent . . . on the life-giving truths of Protestant Christianity. However, when I say religious training I do not mean sectarianism." For Page, "there is a common ground we can occupy." That common ground was a nonsectarian, pan-Protestant approach to education that echoed Lancaster's idealism.

THE NEED FOR PUBLIC FUNDING OF SCHOOLS

Because Lancaster advocated for nonsectarian public schools and taught poor children, he confronted the problem of funding. Throughout his career as a teacher and educational entrepreneur, he faced enormous financial difficulties.

In fact, he was once jailed in a "debtor's prison" because of nonpayment of his bills. Lacking both a secure source of revenue from either tuition or a supportive religious institution, he typically had to rely on philanthropy for support.

PUBLIC FUNDING FOR SCHOOLS

As a result, Lancaster spent a great deal of energy and time raising money for his schools. In fact, the endless struggle to support his schools was a lesson that future educators certainly would understand. As we will see, Horace Mann was particularly concerned with public funding of schools in Massachusetts, and he recognized that only through a steady source of revenue from the state could public education survive.

The lesson, ironically provided by Lancaster's monumental struggle—and failure—to provide a consistent source of funding for his nonsectarian public schools, opened the door to the idea of a tax-supported system of finance.

THE GRADED SCHOOL

One of the more lasting contributions of the Lancaster method of instruction was the placement of students in "classes" according to their ability. This concept is one of the cornerstones of the modern school.

As with other educational innovations, Lancaster broke with tradition. Although the idea of placing students in "classes" had its roots in some Elizabethan England schools and in fifteenth-century French grammar schools, most elementary school children of the early nineteenth century were taught as a group, irrespective of their age or ability level.

Students were given the same lessons to read independently or with a partner. Each student then recited the same material to the schoolmaster. In the United States, where elementary schools were small, terms were short, and books were scarce and often were shared, this method was nearly universal.

THE MONITORIAL SYSTEM

Lancaster's pedagogy, however, was based on both pragmatic circumstances and an "imaginative pedagogical application." Given the fact that he often enrolled two to three hundred students or more, he was compelled to "classify" students of various ages and skill levels into small groups.

Early on he divided his students into groups of ten to twelve "whose proficiency [was] on par" and then assigned each "class" a student "monitor" to provide instruction, maintain discipline, and assess individual student's progress through examinations. This method employed both peer teaching through monitors and a class-based pedagogy.

Lancaster codified this system in his *Pocket Manual* published in 1827. His system, as he referred to it, was designed to provide a kind of "standardized" pedagogy that could be easily implemented by both experienced and beginning teachers. His goal was to transcend what he saw as the dramatic variations in teaching style and the "Master's vague, discretionary, uncertain judgment." This was a system that could be used by all teachers.

SIMULTANEOUS INSTRUCTION

Related to the idea of placing students in classes based on their age and achievement level was the practice of simultaneous instruction—one of the key elements of the modern classroom.

As we have seen, the classrooms of the late eighteenth and early nineteenth centuries were centered on individual reading, memorization, and recitation before the schoolmaster or teacher. Lancaster's innovation of monitors (today known as peer teaching), however, ushered in a new approach that allowed them to teach to an entire "class" of students simultaneously rather than making assignments and then listening to the recitations of individual students, one at a time.

Like other elements of the Lancastrian system, the ideas of monitors and simultaneous instruction were based on a blend of pragmatic circumstance and creative imagination. Lancaster noted that "having no means of paying ushers [I] was compelled to employ one pupil in teaching another." His system, moreover, would "be a guide to his juvenile teachers and render their duties systematic and regular."

Monitors in the Lancastrian schools typically were older, more advanced students selected by the master himself. Each monitor was responsible to teach "simultaneously" the entire "class" in the three basic subjects of reading, spelling, and arithmetic.

EXAMINATIONS

Exposing students, in each proficiency class, to the same material, at the same time, also helped to "level the playing field" of assessment. Moreover, it changed the social relations of the classroom, allowing bright, hardworking students to be rewarded, while the "indolent," as Lancaster called them, were "punished."

This form of assessment was another central element of the Lancastrian school. As Michael Hogan has noted, Lancaster's system of routine examinations created a "hierarchical but continuous structure of opportunity in which the rate of mobility was determined by meritocratic performance."

WRITTEN EXAMS ADMINISTERED REGULARLY

These examinations, moreover, differed fundamentally from older forms of oral, subjective assessment. Most importantly, they were written and "quantitative" in nature. For example, Hogan wrote that while the Jesuits had developed an examination system to evaluate their students, their exams had "no objective mark or grade put upon each piece of work [and therefore] no . . . self validation or perfect [score] . . . and no zero to signify total failure."

Moreover, Lancaster's monitors examined students on a daily basis. At the appropriate time each day, monitors were directed by the master teacher to dictate words or arithmetic problems to their students who would then "write on their slates." When they had completed their test, the signal was given "to the pupils to show slates and to the monitors to inspect them. The examination being finished, the monitors and their assistants returned to their places . . . ready to begin a new lesson."

THE MODERN SYSTEM OF EXAMINATION

In short, the modern system of examinations emerged in the Lancastrian schools. These exams were routinely administered and they were "graded" immediately, thus providing feedback to the students, and they were quantitative in the sense that a specific numeric/letter grade was assigned to their work. Finally, as we shall see, students who did well were praised by both the monitors and their master teacher and they were awarded badges and gifts to signify their success.

Many of the great pedagogues of the nineteenth century borrowed heavily from Lancaster's approach to examinations whether they acknowledged him or not. Edwin Hewitt, for example, wrote that marks for attendance and punctuality "were an essential part of the assessment of students." In addition, "the careful marking of student's scholarship . . . was even more critical." These marks, he went on to say, were an "important written record of the teacher's estimate concerning the relative success of the pupil's efforts."

Charles Northend also wrote extensively of the importance of the written examination. In his classic *The Teacher and the Parent* (1853), he noted "an examination in the prospect should tend to stimulate both teachers and pupils so to perform all their school duties that they will at any time bear a strict and candid inspection."

In other words, the expectation of an upcoming exam would motivate students to study and provide teachers with an instrument to fine-tune their instructional methods, based on the results of the examination.

WHOLE LANGUAGE

In addition to the examination and other instructional and pedagogical contributions, Lancaster introduced what we now know as whole language. This idea would later be used by Emma Willard at her Troy Female Seminary and then by a host of other educators into the twentieth century and beyond.

THE TRADITIONAL "DISCIPLINARY" APPROACH TO TEACHING

Most schools in the late eighteenth and early nineteenth centuries had a "disciplinary" curriculum. Each period of the school day was devoted to a specific subject such as reading, spelling, or writing. Once again, however, the Lancaster method was different. For pedagogical and pragmatic reasons, he combined the study of these subjects into one lesson.

In his biography of Lancaster, David Salmon wrote that the great educator "made many improvements in the field of instruction . . . [including] one practice which seems almost an inspiration, he combined the lessons of reading, writing and spelling." And yet, as Salmon noted, "Today [1904] we are hailing 'Correlation' as the blessed gift of the German Herbart" when in fact this was Lancaster's innovation.

DISCIPLINE

Finally, the Lancaster method of education introduced a radical new form of discipline. Rather than beating pupils with a stick, ferule, or bare hands, he favored a more psychological approach.

Although Lancaster was not the first to reject corporal punishment of students, he helped to popularize the disciplinary ideas of John Locke, Jean-Jacques Rousseau, and other Enlightenment thinkers of the eighteenth century.

EARLY CHALLENGES TO CORPORAL PUNISHMENT

John Locke had first introduced his revolutionary ideas regarding child rearing in his classic work *Some Thoughts Concerning Education*, published in 1705. Locke argued that physical punishment "was the lazy and short way of government [and] the most unfit to be used in education." Rather he favored a system that rewarded good behavior and imposed shame and humiliation for failure and bad behavior.

Lancaster clearly was influenced by these disciplinary ideas. And when he opened his Borough Street School on January 1, 1798, he employed them successfully. He rejected the whipping post (the dreaded symbol of corporal punishment) and instead used incentives such as praise and prizes for success.

LANCASTER'S APPROACH TO DISCIPLINE

For students who misbehaved, had poor attendance, or simply failed an examination, Lancaster used mild humiliation as a powerful method of both instruction and discipline. These punishments included wearing what amounted to a "dunce cap" in the classroom or having a boy's hands washed by a girl in front of the entire class.

In addition to heaping praise on students who had done well on their daily examinations or who had exhibited good behavior in the classroom, Lancaster awarded badges of honor. He also gave these students tickets that could be redeemed for balls, tops, and books.

In 1803 alone, for example, he distributed (out of his own pocket) "five thousand little toys, seven dozen books, twenty-five engraved medals, three star medals, eight silver pens and thirty-six purses."

Once again, Lancaster was not the first to embrace these disciplinary ideas. But by incorporating them into his teaching "system" and popularizing them during his relatively short career, he helped change attitudes toward discipline in the classroom and set in motion a model that would be used in the future.

A CONSENSUS DEVELOPS REJECTING CORPORAL PUNISHMENT

By the middle of the nineteenth century, most treatises on teacher training had rejected corporal punishment in the classroom, preferring more "psychological" approaches. The great educator Charles Northend, for example, writing in 1853, noted that promoting the love of approbation, "the desire to gain the favor of the wise and good and the approval of their teachers," was the surest way to keep order in the classroom.

NATIONAL AND INTERNATIONAL REPUTATION

Lancaster's system was indeed revolutionary. And it wasn't long before he attained great respect from his colleagues, fellow teachers, members of the

House of Commons, and even King George III himself. Following the publication of his *Improvements in Education as It Relates to the Industrious Classes*, he gained considerable fame. He traveled throughout England, gave numerous lectures, and was honored by a special audience with the king.

Then in late 1806, James Pillans, rector of the prestigious Edinburgh High School, wrote that Lancaster's system of education had "converted a laborious and often irksome profession [that is, teaching] into the most easy and delightful employment possible."

The following year on February 9, 1807, he received high praise from a prominent member of the House of Commons. Mr. Whitbread introduced a bill for the reform of England's Poor Laws and in his speech he praised Lancaster by noting that "just within a few years [of the opening of his Boroughs Road School, Lancaster] had discovered a plan for the instruction of youth which has now been brought to a state of perfection." Whitbread went on to say that Lancaster's system of education "will furnish a mode of instruction not only for this country but for all nations."

GREAT INTERNATIONAL RENOWN

This praise was prophetic. Within just a few years, Lancaster had achieved great renown outside his native Great Britain. In fact, by the mid-1830s nearly 1,500 schools bore his name in one form or another and his influence was international, reaching from England, France, Sweden, Denmark, Russia, and Switzerland to Canada, the United States, and Mexico, as well as South American countries such as Ecuador, Colombia, Bolivia, and Peru.

LANCASTER IN THE UNITED STATES

During his relatively short life (he was fifty-nine years old at the time of his death), he enjoyed enormous celebrity. In 1818, he was lured to the United States by the New York Public School Society and went on an extensive lecture tour promoting his new ideas in education.

The governor of New York at the time, Dewitt Clinton, admired Lancaster a great deal and supported his work in both word and deed. As a result, his success in the Empire State was dramatic and he was able to establish schools in New York City, including a very successful one in Brooklyn. In fact, as a testament to his revolutionary educational ideas, Lancaster was given the honor of being "seated" in the New York State House of Representatives.

LANCASTER IN MEXICO AND SOUTH AMERICA

Lancaster gained an even greater international reputation as he traveled to both Mexico and then South America. In Mexico he was hailed as a true visionary, and in 1822 his *compania Lancasteriana* opened many schools.

In fact, five years after his death, in 1843, the *Federal Directorate of Public Instruction* established Lancastrian schools throughout the country. These schools became the foundation of Mexican public education for the next half century.

LANCASTER AND SIMON BOLIVAR

Lancaster enjoyed even more acclaim in South America. In 1825, the great Simon Bolivar (often referred to as the George Washington of South America) invited Lancaster to Colombia with the promise of an enormous grant of $20,000 for the education of children in his country. The great educator now appeared to be in the most secure economic position of his life. As a result, he committed to settle in Colombia and married the wealthy "widow of John Robinson of Philadelphia" who Lancaster noted had a "lovely and interesting family."

LANCASTER MARRIES

The wedding ceremony was a rather lavish affair, though, as might be expected, it was held in one of Lancaster's classrooms. Some of his best students were in attendance and the ceremony was presided over by Simon Bolivar himself, accompanied by his "leading officers and a large party of gentry and merchants."

But the relationship between Lancaster and Bolivar soon soured, and the promised grant of $20,000 never materialized. As a result, the great educator, his wife, and his new family were forced to leave Colombia.

FROM COLOMBIA TO CANADA

Eventually the Lancasters made their way back to New York and then traveled to Montreal, Canada, en route to his native England. Before they were able to depart, however, he received a sizable grant from the Legislature of Lower Canada to establish a school to teach reading to "backward children."

This school operated for only a short time, however, and was closed due to a cholera epidemic. And yet this unfortunate event allowed Lancaster to return to the United States and complete his final book on education, *Epitome* of *Some of the Chief Events and Transactions Containing an Account of the Rise and Progress of the Lancastrian System of Education.*

UNTIMELY DEATH

Then, on a warm late October day in 1838, Joseph Lancaster stepped off the curb on a busy New York street and was run over by an out-of-control horse carriage. The injuries that he received led to the death of one of the most important educational figures of the early nineteenth century.

At the time of his death, however, Lancaster's meteoritic career had already begun to fade. In the somewhat fickle world of education, new ideas were emerging, and there was a growing chorus of criticism from a variety of sources.

CRITICISM OF LANCASTER'S SYSTEM

While his critics grudgingly admired his system for charity schools, most felt it was not appropriate for other students. New ideas by Pestalozzi and Rousseau that recommended a more "child-centered" approach to education had begun to capture the imagination of educators in both Europe and in the United States.

Others such as Horace Mann (who we will turn to soon) criticized Lancaster's monitorial system as superficial and inferior. Mann favored a system in which teachers would receive professional training in "normal schools."

In his *Report on the Educational Tour in Germany* published in 1846, Mann clearly presented this argument: "One must see the difference [he wrote] between the hampering, inexperienced instruction given by . . . a child [monitor] and the developing, transforming and almost creative power of an accomplished teacher."

Established schoolmasters both here and abroad also challenged Lancaster's monitorial system. J. B. Hutton, a schoolmaster from Albany, New York, for example, implored Governor DeWitt Clinton to abandon his support of Lancaster. He wrote that while "the alphabet is indeed taught with great celerity, and I am satisfied that elementary arithmetic may thus be acquired . . . that which requires the exercise of judgment, [cannot be] taught through the medium of monitors."

Still others were critical (perhaps jealous) of Lancaster's success and often called him insane or just conceited. One critic noted by his biographer said, "Lancaster was a man who, if he [found a way] of tying a knot on the end of a thread would have proclaimed aloud that he had made an original discovery destined to regenerate society."

RELIGIOUS OPPOSITION TO NONSECTARIAN EDUCATION

Finally, there was a growing alarm of Lancaster's schools from organized religion. His nonsectarian approach to education, what we have called an essential cornerstone of the modern school, was seen as dangerous by many clerics. Mrs. Sarah Trimmer once wrote of Lancaster's system, "Its cheapness delighted them, its efficiency surprised them, but its excellence in these respects only made it more dangerous—for it was nonsectarian."

LEGACY

Despite these criticisms from educators, politicians, and churchmen, many of Lancaster's ideas inherent in his "system" persisted. As we have seen, he was one of the first to embrace universal education and provide free schooling for thousands of poor young boys and girls who would never have had access to education.

His idea of placing students in small "classes" based on their proficiency was revolutionary. His innovative form of assessment using written exams and assigning grades based on performance was groundbreaking, and his approach to discipline using incentives and rewards while rejecting corporal punishment was pioneering.

Clearly when twenty-year-old Joseph Lancaster open his new school on Boroughs Road on New Year's Day in 1798 he shook the world of education. Despite the great difficulties he faced and the criticism that was heaped upon him during his relatively short career, he helped lay the foundation of the modern school.

Chapter Three

Emma Willard — Women's Education

September 7, 1821

The world of the late eighteenth and early nineteenth centuries was constrained for most American women. Their social, economic, and political worlds were fixed, and typically they were restricted to a life of domesticity. Women had few legal or financial rights either before or after marriage.

Poor white and free black women, on the other hand, had no legal rights, while slaves were chattel property under the law. White, middle-class, and farming women could not own property, and if they did find work outside the household, their wages were not their own. Women could not sign contracts, and it would be another century before they achieved the right to vote through the Nineteenth Amendment.

LITTLE ACCESS TO EDUCATION

Women also had little access to education. A handful of Puritan women were allowed a religious primary education and an even smaller number of young women from wealthier families had the benefit of a governess. The purpose of their education was to prepare them for a life of gentile domesticity.

As a result of these restrictions, most women acquired the lessons of life from their mothers, grandmothers, or sisters. They learned to cook, sew, tend the kitchen garden, and wash clothes by helping in the household. A few learned to read (in order to read the Bible), but they typically were not taught to write—a skill that was the province of men.

Figure 3.1. Emma Willard. Source: Portrait by unknown artist, circa 1805–1815.

THE WORLD OF EMMA WILLARD

It was in this environment that Emma Hart Willard shook the world of education when she officially opened her Female Seminary in Troy, New York, on September 7, 1821. This school was the first female institution that not only offered a rigorous curriculum in traditional academic subjects but also provided teacher training for women.

And while she is not often given credit, Emma also helped launch the "normal school" movement nearly twenty years before Horace Mann opened the first publicly funded teacher training institute in Lexington, Massachusetts.

EARLY LIFE

Emma Hart Willard was born in 1787 into an enormous family, the sixteenth of seventeen children. She grew up on a modest farm in Berlin, Connecticut, and marveled at the stories her father told her and her brothers and sisters about his experiences during the Revolutionary War. It was that sense of adventure and courage that guided Emma throughout her life.

Her father Samuel was a central figure in the Hart family, and when he was not tending the hardscrabble farm, he held regular discussions on the issues of the day and read from the Bible and other books. At an early age Emma took part in these discussions and quickly developed a keen sense of her own identity and purpose in life.

Samuel encouraged all his children to read but took a special interest in his young daughter who had both a fascination and a deep interest in the stories and books he read to the children. Emma was a precocious child, and while she was still a toddler Samuel read to her while she sat quietly on his lap.

EMMA MATURES INTELLECTUALLY

As she matured, Emma became the primary reader in the family, and by the age of ten or eleven had read all the books in the household. These early experiences of reading aloud before her brothers, sisters, mother, and father was an introduction to her brilliant career as a teacher.

In 1802, at the age of fifteen, Emma enrolled in a small academy in Worthington, Connecticut, about a mile from her home. She soon demonstrated her exceptional reading skills and rose to the top of her class, helping other children learn to read and recite.

Two years later, she was offered a position as a teacher during the summer term. This was her first teaching assignment and she excelled at it. By the age of nineteen she was selected as the head of the school and held that position through the winter term of 1806.

SHE'S LEAVING HOME

These early experiences in the classroom prepared her for her new career. She said goodbye to her beloved father and mother and, not yet twenty years old, set out alone to begin teaching. She taught several terms in nearby schools and then traveled nearly two hundred miles to Vermont where she became the principal of the prestigious Middlebury Female Seminary.

THE NEED FOR EQUALITY IN EDUCATION

But her experiences at the seminary were a great disappointment for Emma. Coming from a family where women and men were on an equal footing when it came to academic subjects and informal discussions, the stilted, narrow "curriculum" of Middlebury was stifling for young Emma.

Middlebury, like most other female academies at this time, was little more than a finishing school for young girls. Academic subjects were extremely limited, while sewing, cooking, flower arranging, and music were the core subjects of the school day.

Emma understood that female education should prepare some women for a life of middle-class motherhood, but she also felt strongly that women were intellectually equal to men and should have access to rigorous academic subjects. This, of course, was not available at Middlebury.

MARRIAGE AT AGE TWENTY-TWO

While her two years at the seminary were a disappointment, Emma did meet her future husband, John Willard, during her tenure at the school. John was both a medical doctor and U.S. Marshall for Vermont. Dr. Willard was a fifty-year-old widower with four children and was twenty-eight years her senior. Emma was only twenty-two years old.

Emma married the doctor, moved into his large home, and took care of his children. But her life was difficult during this period. She missed teaching and she felt isolated from the community. She also missed her own family and her new charges thoroughly resented her presence, claiming that she had married their father for his money.

FINANCIAL PROBLEMS FOR THE WILLARDS

Things got even worse for Emma and her new husband in 1812. That year, the Vermont state bank of which John was the director was robbed. As a result, he and the other members of the bank's board felt it was their responsibility to make up its enormous losses. This led to a difficult period for the Willard family, and John was forced to mortgage their home and other properties.

Emma recognized the great financial difficulties of the family and proposed to open a boarding school in their home. At first John objected to the idea, but eventually Emma prevailed and established her own school.

A NEW DIRECTION IN EDUCATION

It was during this period that she struck up a friendship with her nephew John Willard. At that time John was a student at Middlebury College for men and was staying at the Willard home. During their many discussions, Emma became fascinated with the academic curriculum at the college. It also helped reinforce the stark difference between the academic courses available to men as compared to those typically offered to women.

Soon she began to incorporate courses such as mathematics and philosophy into her own curriculum based on the Middlebury College model. This, of course, was a major break from the traditional form of education for women at the time and set the stage for future changes in women's education.

Despite the success of her Middlebury School, Emma continued to have difficulty raising funds. By 1818 she realized that her sources of revenue had virtually evaporated and she looked to New York, a state that was experiencing rapid growth and had the potential for sustained support for her school.

EMMA'S IMPORTANT "PLAN"

To that end, Emma began writing an important pamphlet with the substantial title *An Address to the Public: Particularly to the Members of the Legislature of New York Proposing a Plan for Improving Female Education*. The pamphlet, later published by J. W. Copeland of Middlebury, incorporated many of the ideas she had developed during this period.

And yet the *Plan* was written primarily to encourage support for her school. As a result, it placed special emphasis on the more traditional components of female education: preparing young women for lives as housewives and mothers.

But embedded in this document was Emma's idea to create a school that would also train young women in academic subjects, similar to those of men, and prepare some of them for careers in teaching.

THE STRUCTURE AND CURRICULUM OF THE *PLAN*

The *Plan* focused on both the structure of the school and its curriculum. It recommended that students live at the seminary in small rooms that would accommodate two women. Students would be responsible for keeping their rooms clean and tidy and thus develop their housekeeping skills.

Common areas should also be available for recitation and "apparatus" such as maps, charts, and other materials for science, geography, and other subjects. In addition, the school should have a library that would contain books for instruction and leisure reading, musical instruments such as a piano, as well as some "good paintings" for art instruction.

The curriculum was divided into four parts including religious and moral instruction, literary instruction, domestic education, and ornamental training. In addition, students would be exposed to a system of laws and regulations.

RELIGION AND MORAL INSTRUCTION

The *Plan* called for religious and moral instruction that had a nonsectarian, Christian focus. On the Sabbath, for example, women would spend part of their day listening to "discourses relative to the peculiar duties of their sex." Here Emma would instruct students in their roles as wives and mothers as well as their proper position in the household.

She and her instructors were also expected to lead by example and demonstrate exemplary moral behavior. For example, Emma would read from the Bible each evening while her young students did their sewing.

Special emphasis also was placed on the dress of students. It was to be modest and plain. Clothes typically should be dark in color (Emma always wore black) with no ruffles, lace, or frills—what she called "furbelows."

LITERARY INSTRUCTION

Regarding her literary instruction, Emma wrote that it was important for her young charges to be able to read expressively so that they could interest their children and students in books. Women at the seminary should also be able to explain "natural phenomena" plainly to their children. As an example, she wrote that they should be able to clearly describe why an egg explodes when buried in a fire.

The literary component of the curriculum therefore was central to the academic pursuits of the young women. Science, literature, and later philosophy and geography were all important parts of their course of study.

DOMESTIC INSTRUCTION

Domestic instruction also was vital according to the *Plan*. Students should be able to attend to the duties of the household and provide for the comfort of their husbands and children. Emma wrote that "a spirit of neatness and order should be treated as a virtue." Each morning, time was allocated for students to practice their "housewifery."

A good example of this "housewifery" was Emma's emphasis on "making the bed." Students were required to make their beds each morning and were not allowed to sit or lounge on them. The bed would be inspected by an instructor and must have no wrinkles. Emma recommended that students use a broom handle to "smooth out" all the lumps. Moreover, failure to keep the bed in perfect order would result in a demerit!

Finally, Emma wrote that developing domestic skills was important for students irrespective of their class position. Many of her students would have domestic help once they married, but understanding the importance of neatness, tidiness, and general cleaning of their rooms was essential to the future maintenance of their own households.

ORNAMENTAL BRANCHES

In addition to literary, domestic, and moral education was what Emma called the "ornamental branches." Here she recommended drawing, painting, "elegant penmanship," music, and grace of motion. Needlework, making and mending clothing, and darning socks were also seen as important domestic skills.

Grace of motion was acquired through instruction in dance. Students would dance an hour each day in the late morning. Emma wrote that this provided them with exercise and relaxation and helped them to develop their posture and grace.

Painting and music were also a central part of the ornamental branches. Learning to draw, paint, sing, and play an instrument was integrated into the overall curriculum. While expertise in these areas was not important, developing basic skills was the goal. In this way, women would become well rounded and later, as they improved, they could provide entertainment for their family and guests.

A "SYSTEM OF LAWS AND REGULATIONS"

Finally, students should be exposed to a "system of laws and regulations." This included the general organization of the school along with the established rules and regulations of behavior for both instructors and students. These included qualifications for entrance to the school, the structure of daily life, and the behavior and punishments "to be inflicted on offenders and the rewards for honors to be bestowed on the virtuous and diligent."

EMMA IN NEW YORK

Emma's *Plan* was destined to be a sensation. Two of her students sent a copy to a family friend from New York, General van Schoonhoven. He was so impressed that he promised to deliver the *Plan* to New York governor Dewitt Clinton. Emma then hand copied the entire *Plan* with her best penmanship and enclosed a letter to the governor introducing herself.

The governor was also impressed and assured Emma that he would present her *Plan* to the New York State Legislature for consideration. He followed through with his promise and in his next address to that body he recommended that funds be allocated for women's education in the state.

Emma and her husband John then traveled to Albany, New York, during the legislative session, and she vigorously lobbied numerous lawmakers to support her *Plan* for a proposed school in Waterford, New York.

ANTICIPATION AND DISAPPOINTMENT

Emma was impressive and she felt sure that money would be allocated from the legislature. Later she recalled that "I had . . . determined to go in person to the legislature and plead at the bar with my living voice; believing that I should throw forth my whole soul in the effort for my sex."

As a result of her lobbying efforts, the legislature granted her a charter to establish the Waterford Academy for Young Ladies and also "recommended" a grant of $5,000 to support the school.

But while the charter was approved, the legislature refused to fund the academy. Their arguments against financial support were typical at this time: education for women was considered unimportant and using money from the "Literary Fund" to support her academy would take away resources from the education of young men.

MORAL SUPPORT AND ENCOURAGEMENT

Disappointed but not defeated, Emma agreed to have her *Plan* published. She then sent copies to prominent men throughout the country including President Monroe, Thomas Jefferson, and John Adams.

She gained a great deal of moral support from their responses. John Adams was particularly impressed and sent her a complimentary note. He wrote, "I am deeply indebted to you for your polite and obliging letter and much more for the elegant sentimental and most amiable volume that attended it." He went on to say that "whenever I hear of a great man, I always inquire—who was his mother."

NEW YORK LEGISLATURE REMAINS INTRACTABLE

Despite the overwhelming support from men and women throughout the nation, however, the New York State Legislature remained intractable and funding was not forthcoming. Hoping against hope, Emma and her family along with several of her best students moved to Waterford and opened their academy. There they struggled to survive for three years. But eventually they were forced to close the school because of a lack of capital.

TROY TO THE RESCUE

Seemingly at the last minute, however, Emma received word that that on March 26, 1821, the Common Council of Troy, New York, had passed a special tax allocating $4,000 for her school. Emma had finally found a home.

The Council of Troy purchased an abandoned three-story building that had recently housed the Moulton Coffee House. With twenty-two rooms and a large ballroom, the structure provided more than enough space for the school.

PREPARATION FOR THE SCHOOL

A Board of Trustees was appointed and a "Committee of Ladies" acted as a liaison to the board and regularly conferred with Emma regarding the needs of the school. Meanwhile, the Willards, several instructors, and a handful of students packed their things and moved from Waterford to Troy, where they found temporary accommodations near the site of their new school.

During the summer of 1821 the building was renovated under Emma's constant supervision. She informed the trustees that "I want you to make me a building that will suit my trade . . . and will not complain . . . provided you finish it so that we will not get slivers in our fingers due to rough boards."

A NEW SEMINARY IN TROY

And indeed, the school was completed on time and not one student got a sliver in her finger! When the seminary opened in early September, ninety young women were enrolled in grades nine through twelve.

The excitement concerning the school had spread throughout the country during the spring and summer of 1821, and young women from Massachusetts, Vermont, Connecticut, Ohio, South Carolina, and Georgia, as well as New York, enrolled that first year.

JOHN WILLARD'S IMPORTANT ROLE

Emma's husband John, as usual, was a great help and supported her efforts. He became the business manager of the operation and, of course, the school physician. Although he would pass just four years after the opening of the school, John contributed a great deal to its early success.

THE SCHOOL OPENS

The curriculum of the school followed Emma's *Plan for the Improvement of Female Education* with a dual emphasis on the development of domestic skills along with academic subjects.

In addition, Emma introduced a handful of promising students to the profession of teaching. Besides their basic studies, these women learned some of the new techniques of discipline and instruction.

For example, students were cautioned against the use of corporal punishment on their young charges. This of course was a dramatic break from the typical classrooms of the day where routine violence and public humiliation were used to control young, active children. Using examples from her own teaching, Emma instructed prospective teachers that they should never reprimand students in public but rather talk to them privately concerning their behavior.

READING EDUCATION

Regarding reading education, Emma emphasized comprehension rather than simple recitation. Again the technique of memorization and recitation had been an age-old method of instruction. Reading for understanding and discussion of the reading materials, however, was a new direction in learning and would have a profound effect on education. Later we will turn to the work of William McGuffey and how his famous *Readers* helped to promote this new approach.

A NEW DIRECTION FOR GEOGRAPHY EDUCATION

Emma also introduced the study of geography to her "student teachers." She was so displeased with the quality of geography textbooks at the time, however, that she coauthored two new volumes for use in her classrooms. With William Channing Woodbridge, the noted geographer, she wrote *The Woodbridge and Willard Geographies and Atlases* in 1823.

This volume, as well as a later work titled *A System of Universal Geography*, took this subject into a new and important direction. Most books at that time began with "the study of maps with a map of the world." Often published in England, students were required to memorize the distances of world cities from London.

Emma's work, on the other hand, focused on the United States and began, "in the most simple manner imaginable, to draw a map of her home town." Once students developed a sense of place they could then progress to the study of wider geographic areas.

A NEW VISION OF MATHEMATICS AND HISTORY

She also introduced mathematics to her charges. This subject traditionally had been denied to women because it was thought to be too complex for them to comprehend. Emma bristled at this idea and initiated a series of courses in higher math.

Because there were few books devoted to these subjects, Emma took a page from the work of Pestalozzi and used everyday objects to demonstrate mathematical concepts, especially in plain and solid geometry. She cut out paper triangles and other objects to give them a concrete understanding of shapes. In solid geometry she carved globes, cones, and pyramids out of turnips and potatoes.

Emma also authored a history text titled *A History of the United States or Republic of America* in 1828 and used it extensively in her classes. This book was a patriotic vision of the history of the United States and was written so that her students would begin to understand the development of our political institutions.

WHOLE LANGUAGE

But rather than studying history, geography, and literature in isolation, Emma introduced an innovative method we now know as "whole language." For example, ancient history, ancient geography, and the *Iliad* were studied together.

Later the prolific Emma Willard would write a diverse set of books for students, including a treatise on blood circulation in 1846 and one titled *Morals for the Young* in 1857.

PROMOTING FEMALE EDUCATION

Emma's reputation as a leader in the field of teacher education grew rapidly. Her mere signature on a teaching certificate became the gold standard for teaching excellence. Dozens of her students took teaching positions, while others had become principals of teacher training schools across the United States. Their work helped to transform the image of the female teacher in our culture.

Hoping to expand female teacher education even further she founded the Willard Association for the Mutual Improvement of Female Teachers. As president of the group, she encouraged women to improve their teaching methods, continue their education, and work toward self-improvement. The efforts of this and future organizations such as the NEA, founded later in the century, helped to elevate teaching into a respected profession.

A VISIT FROM LAFAYETTE

Emma's Troy Female Seminary matured during these early years and developed a national reputation. But just three years after its founding, the school gained an international audience with a visit from the Marquis de Lafayette during his grand tour of the United States.

Lafayette, the last surviving general of the American Revolutionary War, arrived in the United States in August 1824. He received a hero's welcome and toured several major cities in the fall of that year.

He visited John Adams at his home in Quincy, Massachusetts, and later visited the White House to meet with President Monroe. He traveled to Mt. Vernon to pay homage to George Washington and went to Monticello to meet with Thomas Jefferson. In short, Lafayette met with former and contemporary leaders of the nation and became a national sensation.

LAFAYETTE VISITS THE SEMINARY

Following his trip to New York City in September 1824, he traveled up the Hudson River and landed in the thriving town of Troy, New York. The citizens of the city gave him a royal welcome and then he was introduced to Emma Willard on the steps of the seminary.

For months, Emma and her students had been looking forward to and planning for Lafayette's visit. He was greeted by the students with a song of welcome written by Emma herself. Then two of her students, both daughters of the current governors of Michigan and Vermont, stepped forward and presented the general with a copy of *A Plan for Improving Female Education*! Lafayette, it was said, had tears in his eyes.

The general shook the hand of each of the students, thanked them for their welcoming song, and then toured the school with Emma. It was during this tour that they spoke about the importance of female education. This conversation clearly made a deep impression on him. Following a brief ceremony, Emma escorted Lafayette through the flower-covered arbor on the grounds to the street where the general departed for Philadelphia.

Though his visit to the seminary was short, it had a dramatic effect on Lafayette. He read Emma's *Plan for the Improvement of Female Education* over the next few months and was quite impressed. In addition, he personally wrote Emma requesting three copies of the song she had written for the occasion to give to each of his three daughters.

A LASTING FRIENDSHIP WITH LAFAYETTE

Near the end of his exhausting year-long tour, Lafayette made a special effort to return to Troy, New York, and once again met with Emma at the seminary. The second visit cemented their relationship and was the beginning of a long correspondence.

When the general returned to France in early September 1825, he heaped praise on the United States and the cordial and enthusiastic welcome that he had received. He had met with the great leaders of the United States, both past and present, participated in numerous parades in his honor, spoke to gatherings of both ordinary citizens and dignitaries throughout the country, and he even received special honors on his sixty-eighth birthday at the White House. But he never forgot his visit to the Troy Female Seminary.

Emma and Lafayette corresponded for the next decade, and he always signed his letters to her as "your affectionate and grateful friend." They often discussed the importance of female education. Emma invited his three daughters to attend the seminary, but the general decided that they should stay in France. He thanked her for this invitation but wrote that he could not bear to part with them.

Emma's reputation grew dramatically during these years. Her seminary became highly respected throughout the world not only as an institution of higher learning for women but also as an innovative teacher training institute.

EUROPEAN TRAVEL

As the seminary grew in both size and complexity, Emma gradually delegated many of its functions to others, including her sister, nieces, and later her son John and his two daughters.

This gave her time to travel, lecture, and write. She went to Paris and met with Lafayette and his daughters. She was then presented at court and honored by the king of France himself. She observed female educational institutions throughout Europe, though she was disappointed with their overall quality.

Following her return to the United States, she gave numerous talks to groups on the importance of female education and continued her writing. She of course retained close ties to the seminary until her death on April 15, 1870.

EMMA WILLARD: EARLY FEMINIST?

Although Emma was not considered to be a feminist during her long career, arguing that women should not engage in politics, she was a strong advocate of the intellectual equality of men and women.

Her lifelong work promoting female education equal to that of men was remarkable in the early years of the nineteenth century. But her curricular development of female teacher training two decades before the first "normal school" was established by Horace Mann in 1839 places her in the pantheon of great educators.

Clearly, Emma Hart Willard shook the world of education on September 15, 1821. It would never be the same!

Chapter Four

Horace Mann—Father of the Common School

June 29, 1837

By the early 1830s, the United States had grown both politically and economically. As a country, it had endured the growing pains of revolution and the process of nation building during its constitutional crisis of the 1780s. It had experienced political upheaval in the early nineteenth century as well as major war with England in the early 1800s.

It had embraced a new free market economic system and during the 1820s it experienced its first Industrial Revolution. The United States had now positioned itself to become the world's most powerful economic nation in just a generation.

These major changes also led to significant demographic transformations as thousands of immigrants from northern Europe streamed into the United States seeking religious and political freedom as well as economic opportunities.

A NEW VISION FOR SCHOOLS

Americans soon realized, however, that these changes also demanded a new approach to education. U.S. reliance on sectarian religious schools, private academies, and tutors may have appeared to work during the colonial and early national periods but were now hopelessly inadequate.

The United States needed a new approach to education that would prepare students for its emerging industrial-based economy and provide them with a sense of national pride and common purpose.

Figure 4.1.   Horace Mann. Source: Mathew Brady Studio, circa 1849.

It was during this exciting era, on a late June day in 1837, that Horace Mann shook the world of education by becoming the state of Massachusetts's first secretary of education and essentially launching the common school movement in the United States.

Mann had little formal connection with education. But while he had never entered a classroom as a teacher or an administrator, his diligence and persistent support of public education during his twelve years in this position transformed our world.

HUMBLE BEGINNINGS

As with many of the great figures discussed in this book, Horace Mann was not "born into greatness." Rather he came from humble beginnings and struggled to make a name for himself.

His father was a poor farmer from Franklin, Massachusetts, and the family lived a very modest life. Horace and his brothers were taught the basics of farming by their father, Thomas Mann, while his mother and sisters attended to the domestic duties of the household.

FAMILY TRAGEDY

Because his father had contracted tuberculosis when Horace was just a child, the family had stoically understood that Thomas would be with them for only a short time. Then, just before his fourteenth birthday, his beloved father died. Horace, now in early adolescence, looked to his mother and especially his older brother Stephen for guidance.

But the following summer, tragedy again struck the Mann family. On a warm Sunday morning, July 22, 1810, Stephen went to the nearby Uncas Pond for fishing and swimming. Later that day, when he did not return home, a search was conducted, and the tragic news was reported to the family: Stephen had drowned.

The death of both his father and older brother within a year of each other had a profound effect on Horace. His other brother, Stanley, had essentially disengaged from the family earlier to become a successful part owner and manager of a new textile mill near Franklin.

EDUCATION: A "WAY OUT" FOR HORACE

This left Horace to tend to the family farm. And although many saw the hard work of an independent yeoman farmer as both admirable and virtuous, for young Horace, it was little more than back-breaking labor with no future.

Rather Horace looked to education as his "way out" from the drudgery of farm life. For years, he had admired the young boys in town who had made their way to Brown University, just thirty miles south of Franklin. Once he made the decision to attend Brown, Horace turned to his studies with renewed vigor, in preparation for his entrance exams.

PREPARING FOR HIS ENTRANCE EXAMS

His focus of independent study now centered on Latin, Greek, and mathematics. Eventually he sought the help of Samuel Barrett to tutor him in Cicero and Vergil. For mathematics he turned to Reverend William Williams, a Baptist. (This was unusual because Horace had been raised as a Calvinist.) Williams had helped other local boys make the transition from farm to university, and Horace benefitted greatly from his advice and instruction during these years.

It's important to remember that until the age of twenty, young Horace had never attended school more than one short term a year. Hard work on the farm gave him little time for the luxury of continuous education at a private school, much less the direction of a tutor.

Rather Horace studied on his own and was a frequent visitor to the local Franklin Public Library. It was here that the world of books fascinated him, and he read voraciously. At the age of twenty, benefitting from the help of both Samuel Barrett and Reverend Williams, Horace was ready for his new intellectual journey

BROWN UNIVERSITY

In 1816, young Horace traveled to Brown University in Providence, Rhode Island, where he would take his formal entrance examinations. As he left his friends and family in Franklin, he was both excited and fearful. Nevertheless, he made his way to Providence and arrived at the school ready for his next challenge.

GRUELING ENTRANCE EXAMS

Horace's exams were grueling. Shortly after he arrived on campus, he was ushered into President Asa Messer's office and examined in "general knowledge." He was then required to translate a portion of the "Greek Testament," an important fourth-century version of the New Testament of the Bible.

Once he had completed his translation, Professors Calvin Park and Jasper Adams entered the president's office and required Horace to translate a selection from Virgil. When this ordeal was completed, Horace was informed that while he had some "deficiencies," he had passed his exams and was admitted to the school as a sophomore.

A NEW DIRECTION FOR HORACE

Three years later, he graduated from Brown with honors. His valedictorian address revealed his future direction as an educator. The essence of this idealistic oration titled "The Progressive Character of the Human Race" centered on the advancement of humanity through the power of education, philanthropy, and republicanism.

Fresh from his brilliant university career, Horace studied law independently, supported himself as a Latin and Greek tutor to the children of a wealthy Massachusetts family, and then became a librarian at his alma mater. About the same time, he began his formal study of the law at Litchfield Law School, and in 1823 he was admitted to the bar in Dedham, Massachusetts.

ACTIVISM AND POLITICS

During the next few years, Mann worked as an attorney but remained an active reformer, especially in his support of the humane treatment of the insane. This would become his early passion, and eventually he was able to help establish an asylum in Worcester, Massachusetts, where he became the chairman of the board.

Mann soon took his reform fervor into politics, and in 1827 at the age of thirty-one, he was elected to the Massachusetts State Legislature as a representative. During the next eight years, he dedicated himself to the social/reform issues facing the state at the time.

REVISION OF STATE STATUES

In addition to his social activism, Horace was involved with the revision of the Massachusetts State Statutes. During the summer of 1835, he edited the entire corpus of state laws and provided detailed marginal notes to assist with judicial review.

This monumental task caught the attention of political leaders throughout the state, and Horace was personally thanked by the statute revision committee for his "faithful, laborious and dignified discharge of . . . duties."

STATE SENATOR

Mann's reputation had grown so rapidly during this period that in the fall of 1835 at the age of thirty-nine he was elected to the Massachusetts State Senate. Within a year, he was selected as president of that body. Later he became the majority leader of the Whig Party and played an important role in promoting infrastructure development, especially the construction of canals and railroads in the state.

PERSONAL TRAGEDY

Throughout this period, however, Mann struggled mightily with depression over the loss of his bride, Charlotte Messer, who had died at the age of twenty-three, just two years after their marriage in 1830. Five years after her death, Horace recorded in his journal a poignant poem that revealed grief for his lost bride: "Oh, Charlotte dear departed shade, look from the place of heavenly rest, seest thou, thy lover laid her rest thou the groans, that rend his rest?"

Soon thereafter he again wrote of his own anguish: "when, oh when will it cease?" Indeed, Horace never fully recovered from this loss, though he would marry his beloved Mary Peabody in 1843 and raise a fine family.

SECRETARY OF THE STATE BOARD OF EDUCATION

The fundamental turning point in Mann's life (and one that shook the world of education) came in 1837 when Massachusetts created a State Board of Education and selected Horace Mann as its secretary.

Mann's interest in establishing a common school in Massachusetts was part of his vigorous support for a wide range of reforms during this period. He had pushed for funds to be allocated for common schools during the 1836 legislative session but had been rebuffed by his colleagues.

He then promoted the idea of a State Board of Education that would simply collect information on the state of education in Massachusetts. Governor Edward Everett supported this modest proposal, but once again it was opposed by legislators by a two to one margin.

VICTORY FOR THE COMMON SCHOOL

Eventually, with the support of his Senate colleagues, sentiment for the creation of the board grew, and in April 1837 the proposal was passed and signed by the governor.

The new law directed the governor to appoint an eight-member board to select a secretary. The board included the most prominent politicians and business leaders in the state, and they recommended Horace Mann for that position.

Although Mann was honored by their offer, he hesitated to accept it. His career in the Senate was on the rise, and it appeared that he was in line to become the Whig candidate for governor of the state one day.

INDECISION AND ACCEPTANCE

For over a week, Mann was in a quandary. He was so conflicted that he had difficulty working and recorded in his journal, "count that day lost, whose low, declining sun, views from thy hand, no worthy action done."

Finally, after much agonizing, on the very last day before a decision had to be made by the committee, he accepted the nomination. The board met and quickly confirmed Horace Mann as the Secretary of the Board of Education.

Despite his initial reluctance, Mann met this challenge head on. Over the next few years he would visit nearly every public school in the state and meet with both teachers and students. Two years into his mighty crusade he established the *Common School Journal* that articulated his vision for the future of education.

PREPARING FOR HIS NEW POSITION

Following his appointment, Horace spent the next two months preparing for his new position. He read a number of works on education, including James Simpson, an English advocate for public education. He was also profoundly influenced by Victor Cousin's *Report on the Prussian School System*.

He consulted back issues of the *Journal of Education* and the *North American Review*. In addition, he studied "town reports" on education from communities throughout Massachusetts. The results were stunning.

THE POOR STATE OF SCHOOLS

For example, in Westport, Massachusetts, a teacher reported that she taught fifteen students in a fourteen-by-sixteen-foot room. In Tyringham, another teacher reported that the school was in "good" condition but noted that she taught seventeen students in a fourteen-by-eighteen-foot room.

Many schools reported that they had no "outhouses," while in Taunton, Massachusetts, the report simply read, "inconvenient benches, a clumsy desk . . . bare walls—no maps—no other apparatus . . . save the switch or ferule." The depressing condition of schools left Mann with despair but also a renewed sense of the importance of public support for the common schools in the state.

AN INTELLECTUAL TURNING POINT— THE AMERICAN SCHOLAR

Just days before Mann delivered his first official speech as the Secretary of Education, he attended a lecture by Ralph Waldo Emerson on August 31,

1837. This pivotal moment in the intellectual life of the nation also had a dramatic impact on Mann and reinforced many of the progressive reform ideas he had held for years.

The title of the lecture was "The American Scholar." In it, Emerson challenged his audience and the nation to take part in a new, exciting period in American history. It was time, Emerson noted, that Americans step up to their rightful place in the world.

Our day of dependence was over, he declared! Our long "apprenticeship to the learning of other lands" had come to an end! America's time had come. This new era would not be built on the foundation of European culture but rather a new sensibility that centered on the strengths of our nation.

EMERSON: "I EMBRACE THE COMMON"

For Emerson it was neither the ancient class system nor the powerful nobility of Europe that would lead the world of tomorrow, it was the common man. Emerson orated this powerful idea by saying, "I ask not for the great, the remote, the romantic . . . I embrace the common, I explore and sit at the feet of the familiar, the low."

These words inspired the nation and had a profound effect on the young Horace Mann who was now on the threshold of an exciting career in education. In this spirit, Mann sought a "new form of education for Americans, one that would reach the rich and the poor alike and . . . promote a common educational experience."

ELEVATING EDUCATION INTO THE REFORM AGENDA

In so doing, Mann incorporated education into the powerful reform agenda of the day, transforming it from a tangential issue into a central component of "the movement." Along with women's rights, temperance, human rights, and abolition, education was now near the top of the national reform agenda.

Reformers of every sort from all over the country soon began to see universal education as a mainstream issue. This was one of Horace Mann's most powerful legacies.

ADVANCING HUMAN WELFARE THROUGH EDUCATION

As Mann began his quest, he realized that the job was enormous, and he called upon all members of society to participate in this grand experiment. In the second volume of the *Journal*, for example, he welcomed all those who were enlisted in "the great cause of advancing human welfare through the . . . perfect education of the whole people."

But Mann also understood very well that not everyone supported the idea of the common school. As such he felt that it was his responsibility to educate the people about the importance of public education. With this task he was a master.

THE ABSOLUTE RIGHT OF EDUCATION

Horace Mann clearly understood the typical arguments against the support of public education. The rich man with no children, he noted, may argue that he should not have to pay for the schooling of others, while the poor man who had never sent his children to school might argue that he should not have to pay to educate his neighbors. Still others who had already sent their children to an academy or had them tutored privately often saw this support of public education as a dual tax.

His response to these arguments provides the fundamental basis of the responsibilities of individuals to the republic. He noted in 1846 that "I believe in the existence of a great . . . immutable principle of natural law—a principle of divine origin which proves the absolute right of education to every human being."

He continued by saying, "there is no such [greater] parsimony as in neglecting the proper culture of youth because of its cost. The real 'spendthrift' in society showers material goods on children but fails to consider 'their heads and hearts.'"

HORACE MANN'S FUNDAMENTAL PROPOSITIONS

Over the course of the next few years, Mann identified several "fundamental propositions" that would illustrate the essential nature of free education for U.S. society. First and perhaps most important was that education was necessary to create a virtuous public citizenry that would sustain U.S. political institutions.

Public education, he wrote, must be supported by the people, not only financially but through their cooperation with teachers and administrators.

EDUCATION: A SOLUTION TO SOCIETAL AND ECONOMIC PROBLEMS

Mann's second proposition was pragmatic. He argued that individuals, who had been deprived of an education and therefore the ability to support themselves, would often turn to crime. In short, the commonwealth would save on taxes to support prisons if education was available to all.

In the same context, he noted that education was essential to the development of the industrial economy. Individuals needed discipline, often developed in the classroom, to understand the rigors of the industrial workplace. They needed basic skills in reading and math to move up the occupational ladder and to be productive in this new economy.

EMBRACING DIVERSITY

Mann's third fundamental proposition was the importance of a common school education that embraced children of all religious, social, ethnic, and cultural backgrounds. By exposing all children to different cultures and ethnicities, he argued, they would begin to appreciate the importance of common citizenship and develop tolerance for diverse points of view and perspectives. This was the essence of the "common school experience."

THE NEED FOR SECULAR EDUCATION

His fourth principle was the need for secular education. Like Rousseau and Lancaster before him, Mann argued that religion and public education must remain separate. Moral teachings should not be ignored in the curriculum, but they must be presented in a nonsectarian manner.

Rousseau also had argued that secular education was appropriate because the contradictory directives from the religious community and those of the state might confuse students. Mann took this argument further by focusing on diversity within the common school. Because students came from different cultural, ethnic, and religious backgrounds, he argued that sectarian religious education was not appropriate.

A PAN-PROTESTANT APPROACH TO MORALITY

And yet he also noted that the curriculum of the common school should embrace a set of moral values. Reading instruction, for example, should promote a nationalistic, pan-Protestant vision of America that would emphasize the moral responsibilities of the individual to God and country.

And in a society that was predominately Protestant in nature, this approach was successful. There was trouble ahead, however, as American society became more diverse and transcended its Protestant roots.

REJECTION OF CORPORAL PUNISHMENT

Mann's fifth principle was his rejection of corporal punishment of children. Like Rousseau before him, who perceived children as free and moral at birth, corrupted only by society, Mann was opposed to the idea of using physical violence on students to enforce righteous behavior and instill discipline.

Rather, he argued, a common school education should reflect the freedoms inherent in American society. As such he rejected the harsh discipline of the Calvinist model of education that had dominated education since the time of the "Old Deluder law" that had established schools in New England during the early 1600s.

THE PEDAGOGY OF LOVE

The "pedagogy of love," as he called it, was his preferred method of both discipline and instruction. Moreover, it presaged his belief that women were the most appropriate teachers, especially in the primary grades.

The acceptance of women teachers had been growing during this period, and more women were receiving a better education. Several female academies, such as Emma Willard's Troy Seminary, established in 1821, had also begun to prepare women for the profession of teaching.

Just a few years after Horace Mann articulated his "pedagogy of love," Alonzo Potter, the great educator, made a strong case for women in the classroom. He noted that because the era of the whipping post and rod for punishment was coming to an end, women were "preeminently qualified to administer . . . a moral influence on children."

CONSOLIDATION OF STATE CONTROL

In addition to these important propositions regarding the common school was Mann's effort to consolidate the power of the state over local school districts. In this regard, Mann was quite successful, and he helped place American education on a path toward further consolidation and state control in the decades to follow.

When Horace Mann took office as the secretary of education in 1837, he had little experience in education and little power to initiate change. The law that placed him in this position was vague. It created a Board of Education but beyond that had avoided the issue of state control of education.

LACK OF SUPPORT FOR PUBLIC EDUCATION

However, he soon began to understand the need for further centralized control of state common schools. His experience in the humble classrooms of his youth and the pathetic state of schools of the day demonstrated the need for a continuous funding source.

But his early call for support of education often fell on deaf ears or was vigorously opposed. In addition, the vocal resistance of the Boston schoolmasters who defied his plans for curricular change and testing all suggested that greater state control of education was needed.

THE PRUSSIAN EDUCATIONAL SYSTEM

Six years after taking office, Mann traveled to Europe to observe their schools. He visited several nations including Belgium, Holland, Scotland, and England. But it was in Prussia that he found a centralized system of education that fascinated him. And it was the Prussian system that he would attempt to replicate in Massachusetts schools.

Prior to the ascension of Frederick the Great in the late 1700s, Prussian schools were virtually nonexistent. The country was poor, most of the people were still in a medieval state of peasantry (bondsmen), and the country was in shambles.

Frederick instituted many reforms, freed the bondsmen, and reorganized the political structure of the nation. But it was Frederick's *Generalschulreglement* Decree of 1763 that led to the creation of Prussia's new school system.

This centralized educational system required that all Prussian children (boys and girls from five to thirteen years of age) be educated in state/municipality-funded schools. This tax-funded school concept certainly appealed to Mann, who had struggled to convince citizens of the importance of universal common schooling.

THE PRUSSIAN EDUCATIONAL LADDER

Beyond the idea of tax-funded schools, Mann also admired the general structure of the Prussian school system itself. This model was a true educational ladder. It consisted of an eight-year primary education or *Volksschule* that introduced students to basic skills such as reading and writing but also music and moral education that emphasized sobriety, duty, and discipline.

The *Realschule* followed primary school, providing a secondary education for Prussian students. Here subjects such as reading, math, and writing were expanded and typically another language, usually French, was introduced.

Once their *Realschule* education was completed, talented students went on to the *Gymnasium*, where they prepared for university study, while others would pursue a trade through apprenticeship.

In short, Horace Mann was impressed with the Prussian tax-supported nature of schools, the concept of "compulsory education," and the educational ladder leading to either a university education or a trade.

PRUSSIAN TEACHER TRAINING

He also was impressed with their professional teacher training system as well as their recognition of teaching as a profession. Finally, Mann admired Prussian national testing of all students and their standardized curriculum for each grade level.

While Mann could not hope to incorporate all these Prussian educational reforms, he now had a template with which to implement many of his philosophical ideas. Tax-supported education was the centerpiece of his reform agenda, but a standardized approach to the curriculum and testing in the schools also became a priority for him.

THE SHIFT TO STATE CONTROL OF EDUCATION

Even more important, however, was state control of education. The local public schools scattered throughout the Massachusetts countryside provided an uneven and poor education for young people. Education in his state and throughout the northern United States had traditionally been funded and implemented by local communities. This had been the model in this country since the passage of the Tenth Amendment to the U.S. Constitution in 1783.

STATES FAIL TO SUPPORT EDUCATION

The Tenth Amendment essentially deferred to the states all the powers that had not been strictly identified in the U.S. Constitution. And because education had not been mentioned in the Constitution, by default states assumed control of their educational systems.

But early on, states were not interested in education and often failed to build schools or hire teachers, deferring to private schools, academies, and tutors to provide an education for their children.

A GROWING DEMAND FOR BETTER SCHOOLS

By the beginning of the nineteenth century, however, the needs of the emerging industrial economy had begun to make education a priority in the United States. Workers, statesmen, factory owners, and even a new class of commercial farmers had begun to demand better schools to offer opportunities for their children and provide skills for the new emerging market economy.

It was in this environment that Horace Mann began his common school crusade. The uneven nature of local schools, their lack of basic supplies such as slates and books, as well as the scarcity of trained teachers had plagued local education for generations.

So when Mann returned from his European tour in the fall of 1843, his head was full of new ideas that would transform public education in his state. State control of education along with a more standardized curriculum and an educational ladder was an emerging reality.

NORMAL SCHOOLS

In addition to these new ideas, was Mann's focus on teacher education. As an ardent supporter of teacher preparation, Mann was responsible for the development of the state-supported normal school movement not just in Massachusetts but throughout the United States.

Mann had been a severe critic of the Lancaster monitorial system that had been popular during the first two decades of the nineteenth century. He understood that the popularity of this system was due in large part to the parsimony of the public regarding the funding of education.

The idea that one teacher, with the assistance of a handful of untrained "monitors," could instruct upward of two hundred children in one large class appealed to many Europeans and Americans.

MANN'S VISION OF TEACHER TRAINING

Mann dismissed this system as nonsense. He argued that teachers must be trained in subject matter, pedagogy, curriculum, and disciplinary techniques to be effective. The Lancaster method, he noted, reduced education to "mere mechanical repetitions without any culture either of the heart or of understanding."

During his trip to Europe in 1843, Mann confirmed his ideas regarding the "inferiority" of the monitorial system and noted that in Prussia, "where the subject of education is best understood, the Lancastrian system of instruction is most condemned."

PUBLICLY FUNDED NORMAL SCHOOLS

One of Mann's first official actions as secretary of the Massachusetts Board of Education was to help establish a publically funded normal school in the state. Along with noted educator Cyrus Peirce, Mann traveled to Lexington, Massachusetts in 1839 and opened the school with Peirce as its first principal.

At the official dedication of this new normal school, Mann optimistically expressed his vision of teacher training. He orated, "I believe that normal schools . . . are a new instrumentality in the advancement of the race. . . . I believe that without them, free schools themselves would be shorn of their strength and their healing power."

SPREADING THE SEEDS OF NORMAL SCHOOLS

Mann was building on the important work of Reverend Charles Brooks and several educational reformers during this era, including Emma Willard and Edmund Dwight. These individuals had seen the importance of teacher education, and Mann brought their vision to fruition clothed in state support and control.

That same year, a teacher training school was established in Barre, Massachusetts, and yet another, a year later in Bridgewater, Massachusetts. The normal school movement was now officially under way and would play a major role in the development of common school education and teacher training throughout the United States.

The first twenty-six graduates of the Bridgewater normal school, for example, were recruited to travel to other states as far away as Michigan and Illinois and become normal school principals. The seeds of common school education were now being spread to the American West and beyond.

Mann's support of teacher training and normal school education transformed education from a voluntary and haphazard job to a profession. While respect from universities and colleges would develop slowly, today schools and colleges of education are an important part of higher education.

BASIC EDUCATION AND VIRTUE TRAINING

Clearly Horace Mann shook the world of education in many ways. First was his call for a common school experience that would not only instruct students in reading, arithmetic, and writing but also encourage them to understand their role in American society as virtuous citizens.

PUBLIC SUPPORT

Second, Mann demanded public support of education. In fact, a central component of his job as secretary of education was to alert the people of Massachusetts to the importance of the common school. Moreover, he continually articulated his idea of the "immutable principle" sanctioned through "divine origin" that all human beings, rich and poor, have the right to an education.

DIVERSITY

Third, Mann embraced diversity in common school classrooms. Clearly his "common school" was a melting pot for the nation where children of all cultures, ethnicities, and religions could begin to appreciate the rights and responsibilities of virtuous citizenship. Moreover, these children would recognize and accept diverse points of view in a nation based on pluralism.

SECULAR SCHOOLS

Fourth, Mann argued that the common school experience would be a secular one. He had seen the effect of sectarian education in the early Massachusetts schools and recognized that they had tended to isolate individuals and promote a narrow vision of morality for children.

Like Rousseau and Lancaster before him, Mann called for a sort of secular morality in the classroom that would apply to the diverse population of students who were part of the common school.

FEMINIZATION OF TEACHING

Fifth, Mann promoted the "pedagogy of love" for the common school classroom. This included a rejection of the harsh discipline of corporal punishment and the promotion of women teachers in primary schools.

CONSOLIDATION AND STATE CONTROL

Sixth, Horace Mann helped to move public education from its disparate local roots to a centralized state system of education. With this new system he was able to ensure funding through tax support from the state, move toward compulsory education, create an educational ladder from the early grades through colleges and universities, and establish a standardized assessment of students at each grade level.

THE NORMAL SCHOOL

Finally, Mann built on the early interest among educational reformers to create a normal school system to instruct teachers in a standard pedagogy, curriculum, and new disciplinary techniques. The publically funded normal schools established in Massachusetts in the late 1830s and early 1840s provided the essential seeds that would be planted in other communities in the coming decades and helped transform American education.

Horace Mann shook the world of education in June 1837, and his legacy as the "father of the common school" places him in the pantheon of great American educators.

Chapter Five

William McGuffey—The Graded *Reader*

April 1, 1836

As we have seen, the first great era of social reform in America emerged in the early years of the 1830s. A new generation of young men and women had begun to champion such important issues as individual rights, temperance, abolition, women's rights, prison reform, fair treatment of the insane, and, yes, public education.

PROBLEMS WITH EARLY SCHOOLS

Education was far from universal during this period, but the idea of the common school was slowly taking shape in this country. And yet while there was growing interest in public education, school facilities were solely lacking. The quaint image of the little red schoolhouse was a myth—most schools in the 1830s were ramshackle buildings, converted barns, or shacks that were poorly lit and heated.

Beyond these problems, however, was the lack of books. Most students either shared a book brought from home or borrowed one from their teacher. Others read their family Bible.

LACK OF STANDARDIZED READERS

Even in well-appointed schools, such as those in New England or mid-Atlantic cities, the typical reader was some version of the ancient *New*

Figure 5.1. William McGuffey. Source: Unknown artist, unknown date.

England Primer. Otherwise, standardized readers were virtually unknown. Then on April 1, 1836, William McGuffey shook the world of education when he published his first *Reader*.

The common school movement as we know it today was in its infancy, but for it to be successful, a new approach to reading was needed. McGuffey's new *Readers* would transform the way teachers taught and how students learned for generations to come.

EARLY LIFE

Old Guff, as he came to be known, was an unassuming and deeply religious man. And like many others discussed in this book, he came from humble beginnings. William Holmes McGuffey was born in Claysville, Pennsylvania, on September 23, 1800. His parents, Alexander (Sandy) and Anna Holmes, worked a small farm and scratched out a meager existence.

As a young man, Sandy had enlisted in the army to fight Indians in the Ohio Valley. He began as a scout in 1790 and later became part of the regular army. He fought for three years under General Wayne. Their efforts were successful, and the various tribes were routed and forced to sign the Treaty of Greenville in 1795.

Sandy returned to civilian life and eventually met and married Ana Holmes in 1797. Ana came from a successful farming family and grew up on a four-hundred-acre spread outside of Pittsburgh. The young couple moved in with the Holmes family, and Sandy worked the land for his father-in-law. Over the next few years they had three children; their second was William Holmes McGuffey.

A NEW FARM IN THE WESTERN RESERVE

In 1802, Sandy McGuffey struck out in search of a new farm for his growing family. He traveled west to a frontier region of Ohio that he knew well from his Indian-fighting days. He eventually purchased 130 acres of land in the Western Reserve known as Gravel Hill Farm. He cleared a portion of the land and began construction of a log cabin. He then returned to Pennsylvania for his family.

The spectacle of the family traveling west over two hundred miles would have been humorous if it had not been so dangerous. The two older children were placed in baskets and strapped to a horse led by Sandy, while Ana rode another horse and carried the baby in her arms.

Though the country was not quite as dangerous as it was when Sandy fought in the Twelve Tribes Indian Wars in the 1790s, it was treacherous nevertheless. The young family faced wild animals, a harsh climate, and numerous other perils as they made their way to their new home.

GREETED BY A SNAKE

When they finally reached their half-completed cabin, Sandy lit a celebratory fire made of pine knots. But the festivities were interrupted when the family was greeted by a large snake that came slithering into the cabin, having been awakened by the fire.

The next few years were difficult but happy ones for the McGuffey family. They scratched out a hardscrabble existence on their farm, and Ana bore five more little McGuffeys.

Worn out and exhausted by frontier life and the difficulties of bearing eight children, however, Ana passed away at the age of fifty-three. Sandy soon remarried a widow from the region who was twenty-five years his junior, who went on to bear him three additional children.

EARLY EDUCATION

Despite their poverty and the backbreaking work of a frontier farm, Sandy and Ana were determined that young William would receive an education. Early on, Ana recognized that he was a precocious child, and she read to him constantly, tracing letters and figures in the ashes of the fireplace.

When the time came, William enrolled in a small country school near his home in Coitsville, Ohio. But it soon became clear that he had learned all that the teacher had to offer and he needed more advanced education.

A NEW "PATH" TO EDUCATION

The family wanted William to attend Reverend Wick's school in Youngstown, Ohio, five or six miles from their home, but there was no road connecting the two towns. Recognizing the importance of William receiving an education, Sandy and William's grandfather cleared a small path through the woods so that the young boy could attend school.

Once the path was completed, William and his older sister Jane were able to attend school during the winter term and live with Reverend Wick during the week. On weekends the two made the journey back home to Coitsville.

FIRST TEACHING ASSIGNMENT

William learned a great deal from Reverend Wick, and at the age of fourteen he began teaching in a subscription school in what is now called Calcutta, Ohio. His goal was to make enough money so he could continue his education and eventually become a Presbyterian minister.

His first teaching assignment, however, was a disappointment. The long hours, the lack of support from the community, the poor quality of students, and the isolation from his family eventually led him to close the school after four years.

UNIVERSITY TRAINING

Then in 1818, Reverend Thomas Hughes recruited William to attend his Greersburg Academy in Darlington, Pennsylvania. There William lived in the pastor's home and "chored" for his expenses.

William attended the academy for several years and then enrolled in Washington College (later Washington and Jefferson College) in Washington, Pennsylvania. There he earned his bachelor's degree in 1826 with concentrations in Latin, Greek, Hebrew, ancient history, and philosophy.

He was determined to excel in college, but unlike many of his classmates, who came from wealthy families, William was quite poor. To pay tuition, room, and board he taught school when classes were not in session. And yet there often was no money left over to purchase books. As a result, he regularly borrowed books from classmates and copied and bound them by hand for his own use.

AN OFFER FROM MIAMI COLLEGE

It was during one of these early teaching assignments at a private school in Paris, Kentucky, that Reverend Robert Bishop, the first president of Miami College in Oxford, Ohio, heard of William's teaching abilities. Bishop traveled over a hundred miles to Paris and visited William's classroom.

The bishop was so impressed that he offered William a position as professor of ancient languages. His salary was $600 per year, a sum that stunned the young man. Although he had not completed his degree, he accepted the position but continued his studies, graduating in absentia.

HEADING TO MIAMI

The McGuffey family was overwhelmed with joy that their young prodigy had secured a teaching position at a college. Ana gave her blessing but asked only that William promise to complete his studies to become a minister and that ten-year-old Alexander, William's younger brother, accompany him to Miami.

William agreed and in February 1826 the two McGuffeys set out for the college on horseback with their saddlebags filled with books and provisions. They traveled west along the newly opened "national road" and slowly made their way on their three-hundred-mile odyssey.

A HUMBLE INSTITUTION

When the two finally arrived in Miami, they encountered what amounted to a small frontier outpost with a few log cabins and one brick building. They secured lodgings at a local tavern and William began teaching the following term.

The student body at Miami College was quite diverse, with ages ranging from ten years old to men in their mid-thirties. This presented William with a challenge, but he was able to excel once again as a teacher.

MARRIAGE AND FAMILY

During his first exciting year as a professor, William met the love of his life, Harriet Spinning of Dayton, Ohio. Harriet had been visiting her brother, Charles, an Oxford merchant, and the young couple spent several weeks together under his watchful eye.

When Harriet returned home, she and William corresponded and soon their friendship turned to love. After a short courtship, the two were married in 1827 and settled in the small college town. In 1829, following William's ordination as a Presbyterian minister at Bethel Chapel, they moved into a small frame house and began their family. By the early 1830s they were able to purchase a spacious brick home in town, where they raised their five children.

EDUCATIONAL REFORMER

It was during this period that McGuffey's career as an educational reformer developed rapidly. As a champion of common schools in Ohio, he had numerous speaking engagements in and around Miami College and he often lectured in Cincinnati. It was there he met Lyman Beecher and his family in 1832.

The Beechers had recently relocated to Cincinnati from New England and Lyman became the president of Lane Theological Seminary. The family quickly established an intellectual circle that included numerous reformers in the fields of education, abolition, and women's rights. William soon became part of the circle and his reputation soared.

THE CINCINNATI REFORM CIRCLE

In 1836, the distinguished group, included William McGuffey; Catherine Beecher; Catherine's younger sister Harriet Beecher Stowe; author and editor Edward Mansfield, Ohio's first superintendent of common schools; Samuel

Lewis; educational author Albert Picket; and Joseph Ray, author of *Ray's Arithmetic*.

Together they established the College of Teachers as one of the first teacher associations in America. This organization later became the Western Literary Institute, which in turn was the forerunner of the National Education Association.

THE FIRST TWO *READERS*

That same year, 1836, William Holmes McGuffey shook the world of education when he published his first two *Readers* for common school students.

Truman and Smith publishing house of Cincinnati had been looking for a suitable editor for this project for some time. Given the growing excitement over educational reform during this period, they understood that there was a need for a set of standardized *Readers* for young children. Earlier that year, Catherine Beecher Stowe had recommended McGuffey as a suitable author.

McGuffey was offered $1,000 to write and edit the first four *Readers*, a *Primer*, and a *Speller*. He agreed and thus one of the most important sets of common school *Readers* soon became a reality.

What McGuffey created, however, was a sensation and redirected how teachers taught and students learned. The first two *Readers* were published in 1836 and transformed education in three important ways.

REJECTION OF MEMORIZATION

First, McGuffey directly engaged teachers through his "Suggestions for Teachers." In this section, McGuffey encouraged teachers to abandon the age-old method of teaching through memorization.

McGuffey wrote that "nothing can be more fatiguing to the teacher than a recitation." Rather, he suggested that teachers "try the conversational method of communicating instruction and training of the mind." By using the "discussion questions" at the end of each entry, teachers could engage their students and transcend the abstractions of simple memorization.

A CHILD-CENTERED APPROACH TO EDUCATION

Through this method, education slowly moved toward a more progressive, child-centered activity. The primary role of teachers gradually shifted from disciplinarian to facilitator of learning.

Today educational researchers understand that students learn to read not through memorizing rules and passages but by connecting what they know through their own experiences to what they are reading. Through discussion, teachers make the words being processed more comprehensible.

In short, McGuffey's *Readers* revolutionized the way that teachers taught. Rather than simply listening to students recite memorized reading material while others sat on benches desperately trying to memorize their passage, they could begin to engage students through discussion questions from the *Reader*. The shift from memorization to understanding had begun.

COMPREHENSION AND ASSESSMENT

In addition to changing reading instruction from simple memorization to an understanding of the material, the *Readers* opened the door to written examinations.

The traditional method of assessment of student progress had been subjective and informal. Students who had a knack for memorization were often at the top of their class. First-class spellers and spelling bee champions were revered in their communities and often became local heroes of sorts.

MEMORUS WORDWELL

But did these students understand what they were memorizing? Warren Burton, the great pedagogue, provides us with some insight here with the story of "Memorus Wordwell, the Hercules in the wilderness of words."

Burton wrote that Memorus "could spell any word in his speller" but as one of his classmates noted, "he did not know at all what the sounds he uttered meant." Moreover, when Memorus was questioned as to the meaning of the reading material that he had memorized, he failed miserably.

A NEW MEASURE OF ASSESSMENT

As teachers moved from memorization to understanding, students such as Memorus were not necessarily at the top of their class. Now comprehension of the material was important, not simply parroting passages to the teacher.

Certainly the formal presentation of reading material would continue to be an important part of the pedagogy during this period. The classic approach of speech with formal gestures and dramatic effect was considered essential for professions ranging from the law to the clergy and politics.

ARTICULATION, INFLECTION, AND POETIC PAUSES

The *Fifth Eclectic Reader*, for example, addressed this issue by alerting students that "the great object to be accomplished in reading . . . is to convey to the hearer, fully and clearly, the ideas and feelings of the writer." To that end, the *Reader* began with sections on articulation, inflection, accent, emphasis, modulation, and poetic pauses.

It would be years before written examinations would routinely be used in the classrooms of the nation. Nevertheless the door to reading comprehension rather than memorization, recitation, and presentation had been opened.

THE GRADED *READER*

The third and perhaps most important contribution of the McGuffey *Readers* was that they were "graded." McGuffey had begun his teaching career at the age of fourteen and he recognized that his students were often confused, overwhelmed, and discouraged when presented with material that clearly was too advanced for them.

McGuffey understood from his own teaching experiences that while some young students might be able to memorize passages from Shakespeare, Milton, or the Bible, they had great difficulty understanding the material. As a result, he presented material in his *Readers* in a manner that would be understood by students as they progressed through the "grades."

THE ORIGIN OF THE BASIL READER

McGuffey also recommended that teachers use repetition to help students comprehend material more fully. In his early *Readers*, for example, he repeated words in each selection in order to reinforce the material so they could progress to the next "graded" *Reader*.

These ideas were the genesis of the basal readers that emerged in the late nineteenth and early twentieth century. With readers such as the famous *Dick and Jane* series, for example, students progressed from one reading level to another once they had mastered the material. A form of the basal reader remains the centerpiece of reading education today.

A CHALLENGE TO THE *NEW ENGLAND PRIMER*

In addition to the important pedagogical contributions of the *Readers*, McGuffey was able to engage students with an "eclectic" mix of stories, poems, speeches of patriots, and some biblical verses.

McGuffey quietly challenged the early "primers" that had dominated primary reading education from the colonial era to the early nineteenth century. The *New England Primer* (and other primers modeled after it) was the most visible reading volume of these years and was often the only book, other than the Bible, that many American families owned.

THE RELIGIOUS CONTENT OF *PRIMERS*

The *New England Primer* typically included an annotated alphabet, vowel and consonant sounds, and "easie syllables for children" that included 140 combinations. These were followed by words of one syllable, then two-, three-, four-, five-, and even six-syllable words.

Following the "syllabarium" as it was called, the *Primer* presented the famous twenty-four pictures (I and V were not included) with accompanying alphabetical rhymes. Generations of students read and memorized these scriptural and morality-based verses such as "In Adams fall, we sinned all" and "the Idle Fool is whipt at school."

From there, the *Primer* presented the Shorter Catechism, followed by a selection of both short and longer passages from the Bible, including the Lord's Prayer, the Ten Commandments, and a selection of scriptures to be memorized and then recited to the schoolmaster. As we have seen, this was the primary method of reading instruction in America from the colonial era to the publications of the McGuffey *Readers* in 1837.

NATIONALISM AND PLURALISM

Despite McGuffey's deeply held religious beliefs, he also understood the need to provide students with a sense of national identity and civic virtue. The nation was growing rapidly, its economy was changing, and it was becoming more diverse.

McGuffey, like other educational reformers, understood well that the schools must provide students with an introduction to the patriotic values of the nation, as well as a sense of civic virtue and personal responsibility. Schools were the melting pot of the nation!

To that end, McGuffey's *Readers* were a dramatic shift from the early *Primers*. Of the forty-five selections in the first *Reader*, only ten directly mentioned God, while two others referred to the Bible.

INDIVIDUAL RESPONSIBILITY

In his first *Reader*, selections focused on individual responsibility. For example, temperance, a value that was becoming important during this period, was presented in a story titled "Don't Take Strong Drink." In another selection, "The Whisky Boy," students were warned of the dangers of drinking alcohol.

In this selection, little John "got tipsy every day" and by age eight had become a drunkard. Eventually John was found drunk in the street, brought to a poorhouse, and died within two weeks! The lesson ended with a question: "How do you think his father felt now?"

THE VALUE OF KINDNESS

In addition to these warnings, McGuffey included many selections that emphasized the need for kindness among young students. In fact, seventeen of the forty-five lessons in the first *Reader* emphasized this theme. Students were instructed to be kind to all living things, specifically to cows, oxen, cats, dogs, birds, and even flies.

By understanding that cruelty to animals and insects was a sign of selfishness, children would begin to perceive the limits of their own self-interest and understand that there was more to life than what *you* wanted to do.

THE LIMITS OF SELF INTEREST

This value was illustrated in the selection "The Cruel Boy." In this story George Craft liked to pull the wings off flies. It amused him! Eventually another boy explained to him that it was cruel to act in that way even if it was "fun."

McGuffey built on this idea and extended it to a general lesson on kindness to people, especially the sick or handicapped. He then expanded this idea in a number of stories to encourage students to be kind to their friends, brothers, sisters, parents, and teachers.

Two selections from the *First* and *Second Readers* illustrate McGuffey's approach to understanding the importance of kindness to others and the limits of self-interest. The initial entry comes from the *First Reader* titled "Never Do Mischief." Here a group of boys dressed up in white sheets carrying candles and frightened Henry. Henry was traumatized and became an "Idiot." When the boys recognized the consequences of their actions, they were ashamed.

THE GRASS ROPE

A similar theme was expressed in the *Second Reader* titled "The Boys Who Did Mischief for Fun." This story introduces two boys who "did not care whether people were hurt or not, provided they could have a laugh." The boys tied grass together into a rope and stretched it across a path. They laughed as several travelers tripped over the rope. It was fun to "see people tumble on their noses."

They tripped a farmer and then a milkmaid and then a man who was running down the path. When he fell, he sprained his ankle and couldn't walk. But humor turned to horror when they found that the man was on his way to get a doctor to save the life of one of the boy's fathers. The lesson was clear, and the boys never did that again "as long as they lived."

THE PATHETIC MIGRANT

Another tale in the *Fifth Reader* that seems appropriate for today told the story of a group of migrants who were struggling to move from Maine to Illinois. Their poverty seemed to be a joke to many, and they were ridiculed. Then, when their horse broke through a rotten bridge and was drowned, many simply laughed at their plight.

One man, however, gave the pathetic migrants ten dollars so they could continue their journey. The group eventually reached Illinois and their leader became a "thriving farmer and a neighbor to him who was his friend in need and a friend indeed."

RATIONAL OBEDIENCE

In addition to the development of kindness and a subordination of your own self-interest, McGuffey emphasized the importance of obedience—especially to parents. Once children understood this concept, they were encouraged to obey secular authorities such as police officers, members of their town council, government officials, and employers.

Obedience, however, was not to be commanded by a powerful authority but understood in a rational context. In the *First Reader*, for example, obedience and respect for parents was demonstrated in several stories. In "The Walk," for example, a father explains the wonders of nature to his son. In "The Good Girl" a young girl is taught to sew by her mother, and in "How to Add," a mother teaches her children basic arithmetic.

Through these stories, the importance of parents was reinforced and respect for them was a natural response to what they did for them. Again, obedience was not dictated by either the Bible or a secular authority but was derived from an understanding of the importance of parents in their lives.

LOVE OF COUNTRY

While many students left school before the age of ten and thus were exposed to just the first two *Readers*, more advanced *Readers* developed themes that were introduced in earlier volumes. Perhaps the most important of these was a sense of nationalism—love of country.

Stories included in these *Readers* were selected to inspire young students and included many passages on the Founding Fathers such as Paul Revere, Alexander Hamilton, Thomas Jefferson, Benjamin Franklin, and, of course, George Washington.

THE HEROISM OF THE FOUNDING FATHERS

These stories included exciting tales of their accomplishments, including Paul Revere's heroic midnight ride and Washington's famous apocryphal cherry tree incident where he admitted to his father that he had cut down the cherry tree.

In addition to these stories of patriotism, bravery, and honesty were exciting tales of victories in battle. There were also several poems included in the *Readers* selected to inspire students as to the greatness of our country. One selection titled "What I Live For" was read by generations of young students who marveled at the greatness of their nation's history.

> I live to learn their story
> Who suffered for my sake
> To emulate their glory
> And follow in their wake
> The noble of all ages
> Whose deeds crown History's pages
> And Time's great volume make.

AN ASSESSMENT OF THE *READERS*

The McGuffey *Readers* helped to mold young students throughout the nation for generations. Well into the twentieth century students continued to learn the importance of family, community, kindness, obedience, and eventually patriotism.

In a nation that was becoming more and more diverse over the course of the nineteenth century, these *Readers* were important. Students were exposed to a reading curriculum that was both interesting and uplifting. They learned important lessons through rational understanding rather than simply being instructed by a powerful religious or secular authority. And perhaps more importantly, students were exposed to a cultural melting pot that helped develop a powerful and unified nation.

LIMITATIONS OF THE *READERS*

But McGuffey was a product of his era. His attempt to mold a nation of students into god-fearing, patriotic individuals was a noble effort. And yet the *Readers* were flawed. They presented a vision of the nation that was pan-Protestant and white.

As the country developed in the late nineteenth century, the ethnic and racial composition of the nation changed as well. And while the values instilled in generations of young men and women were good ones, they sometimes failed to address the needs of that changing society.

LATER LIFE

McGuffey completed the first of his four *Readers* while he was still a professor at Miami College in Ohio. Then in 1836, he left Oxford to become the president of the newly formed Cincinnati College. It was there he was able to work more directly with the Cincinnati Reform group. Despite increasing enrollment at the college, however, the school failed financially during the depression years following the Panic of 1837.

Then in 1839, McGuffey became president of Ohio University in Athens, Ohio, where he received a substantial salary. While he was president the student population more than doubled and he was respected by both students and faculty alike.

DISLIKED BY LOCAL FARMERS

Despite his success at the college, however, he was unpopular among the local farmers who resented his fencing of the college and the restrictions on public grazing of farm animals on the campus.

Tensions grew and eventually McGuffey was reviled by the local community. He and his family were ridiculed in the local press and he was pelted with mud more than once during his four-year tenure. As the family left Athens, his young son Charlie lost his shoe. McGuffey was heard yelling to the family, "don't look back, I don't ever wish to set eyes on that place again!"

UNIVERSITY OF VIRGINIA

After a short stay in Cincinnati, in 1845, McGuffey was offered a professorship at the prestigious University of Virginia. He became a fixture at the school and taught full time into his seventies. McGuffey died in Charlottesville at the age of seventy-three.

Though he never saw his *Readers* as his greatest legacy, McGuffey shook the world of education with their publication. These unassuming schoolbooks transformed the way that teachers taught and students learned.

He quietly helped to move education from its religious foundation to a more secular learning experience. His books cemented the importance of the common school in the minds of Americans and helped to unify a nation during a transitional period in American history.

Chapter Six

John Dewey—Father of Progressive Education

January 13, 1896

By the end of the nineteenth century, American public education had changed dramatically. The success of the common school had confirmed the importance of primary education for students, and by the mid-nineteenth century the high school movement had began to take shape as well.

COMPLETION OF THE EDUCATIONAL LADDER

With our well-established university system, we had developed the essential elements of an educational ladder. Moreover, the curriculum and pedagogy of both primary and secondary education had been improved by a number of important progressive reformers.

These included Johann Herbart's work that provided teachers with a five-step plan of instruction, William Heard Kilpatrick's "project method" that promoted "socially purposeful acts," and Maria Montessori's concept of student-centered learning through self-directed activity.

While these towering figures and many others introduced new approaches to education, John Dewey was the giant among them. Dewey's passionate embrace of democracy, his concept of "learning by doing," and his understanding of the classroom as a microcosm of the community provided a foundation for a new era of education.

Then on January 13, 1896, John Dewey shook the world of education when he established the preeminent laboratory school in the United States on the campus of the University of Chicago. This school set the standard for

Figure 6.1. John Dewey. Source: Public domain photographs.

child-centered progressive education in America and transformed our understanding of classroom teaching.

IMPORTANCE OF JOHN DEWEY

Dewey had distinguished himself among progressive educators at the time when he was recruited by the president of the University of Chicago, William Rainey Harper. He joined an eminent group of professors at the new school that would soon become one of the most influential universities in the nation.

Dewey was the intellectual bridge between the ideas of Pestalozzi and Rousseau and the neoprogressives of the 1960s and beyond. He built on Pestalozzi's idea that learning could not take place in the abstract, arguing that education must have concrete expression. From Rousseau he developed the notion that learning was possible only when students were interested in the subject.

EDUCATION: MORE THAN BASIC KNOWLEDGE

Beyond these ideas, however, Dewey felt strongly that education was more than the acquisition of basic knowledge. It must also help students reconnect with their community and understand the interdependency of society.

Like many progressives at the time, Dewey was alarmed by the stunning growth of individualism at the expense of community. The nearly universal acceptance of the market economy and the rapid growth of industrialization in the late nineteenth century had created a society that was becoming more and more fragmented and had lost its sense of interconnectedness.

LEARNING BY DOING

Dewey's idea of "learning by doing" helped to address these problems. By immersing students in projects such as building a clubhouse, running a grocery store, or planting a garden, they would begin to appreciate the complexity of our occupational structure and also the importance of collaboration. In this way, students would begin to develop a greater sense of community.

While rooted in the philosophical ideas of Pestalozzi and Rousseau, Dewey's ideas would provide a new path for educators for the next century. His experiments with child-centered progressive classrooms spawned a host of curricular innovations during the neoprogressive period of the 1960s and beyond. These included experiential learning, inquiry-based instruction, preschool education, whole language, the open classroom, and many others.

EARLY LIFE

John Dewey was born in Burlington, Vermont, on October 20, 1859. He was the third son of Archibald and Lucina Dewey. Lucina came from a well-to-do farming family, and Archibald ran a successful grocery store in Burlington.

Archibald had joined the Union forces in 1861 and served his country in combat. When he returned to Burlington, he established a successful tobacco shop. As a result, the family enjoyed a comfortable income and John had access to books and schools.

PUBLIC SCHOOL AND COLLEGE GRADUATION AT NINETEEN

Archibald loved to read and had a penchant for English literature. He read to his sons during their early years and instilled in them a strong sense of the importance of education.

John attended public school in Burlington and was an excellent student. In fact, in 1875 at the age of fifteen he was accepted at the University of Vermont where he distinguished himself as a scholar. He graduated from Vermont at the age of nineteen, second in his class.

FIRST TEACHING POSITION

Following graduation, John's first teaching assignment was at Oil City High School in Pennsylvania. He taught there for three years but struggled with classroom teaching. He then returned to Vermont in 1882, where he taught the winter term at Lakeview Seminary. Despite his keen interest in education, Dewey recognized early on that teaching in the common school was not his forte.

As a result, in the fall of 1882, he enrolled at Johns Hopkins University to begin his graduate education. There he studied philosophy and psychology under G. Stanley Hall, wrote his dissertation on "The Psychology of Kant," and graduated with a PhD in 1884.

TURNING POINT: EUGENICS

This period was a turning point in Dewey's intellectual development. Although he learned a great deal from his mentor Hall, especially the concept of developmental stages in children, he had a fundamental disagreement with him over the idea of eugenics.

As we will see, G. Stanley Hall was a key figure in the development of the eugenics movement. Like other eugenicists, Hall believed strongly that intelligence was inherited rather than developed. He embraced the ideas of Sir Francis Galton and was an early supporter of standardized testing to measure intelligence.

G. STANLEY HALL MOVES TOWARD EUGENICS

As a student at Harvard University, Hall studied the new field of psychology and spent a year in Germany working under Wilhelm Wundt, the noted experimental psychologist. It was here that he became interested in the use of questionnaires to study the human mind.

Following his graduate work, Hall taught at Harvard and then went on to Johns Hopkins where he taught for two years. Here he established the nation's first psychology lab in the United States with the assistance of his student John Dewey.

EARLY TENSION BETWEEN HALL AND DEWEY

But while Hall was quickly embracing the use of questionnaires and eventually standardized tests to sort individuals based on their "intelligence quotient, or IQ," Dewey preferred a more democratic approach to learning.

Dewey believed that all children could learn and through innovative instruction could achieve. Moreover, he welcomed diversity and rejected the notion that certain ethnic and racial groups were inherently inferior to others.

He also felt strongly that all individuals, even those with physical or mental handicaps, could learn as well. As a testimony to that idea, he and his wife Alice adopted a physically handicapped boy they met while traveling in Europe. With access to innovative education, their adopted son Sabino went on to have a successful career in teaching.

AN EMERGING SCHISM IN EDUCATION

The gradual split between G. Stanley Hall and John Dewey—two titans in the field of philosophy, psychology, and education—represented the two sides of a schism in the field of education that continues to this day.

Hall supported the emerging field of standardized testing and the sorting of students into different educational tracks based on their score on these tests. This has become a central feature of some educators today and the foundation of such programs as the infamous "No Child Left Behind."

On the other hand, John Dewey supported democratic, progressive education that embraced diversity. He argued that all children could learn given the proper environment and methods of instruction. Although Dewey did not reject assessment, he viewed "tests" as diagnostic tools that would assist learning rather than sort individuals into different educational tracks.

DEWEY AT MICHIGAN

Following his graduation from Johns Hopkins, Dewey accepted a position at the University of Michigan where he taught from 1884 to 1894 (with a year at the University of Minnesota). It was during his Michigan years that both his personal and intellectual life changed dramatically.

At Michigan he met and married Alice Chipman when she completed her PhB. Together they had six children, though two sons died tragically. Their marriage would end in 1927 when Alice succumbed to complications from a heart attack that she suffered in Mexico City the year before.

Intellectually, Dewey's years at Michigan were productive. He gradually worked his way up the academic ladder, beginning as an instructor in philosophy, then an assistant professor of philosophy, and finally a professor of philosophy from 1889 to 1894.

AN INTELLECTUAL SHIFT TO EDUCATION

In 1886, Dewey published an important textbook titled *Psychology*, the first of its kind in the United States. Then three years later in 1889, he made his distinctive move into the field of education with the publication of *Applied Psychology: Introduction to the Principles and Practice of Education*.

His years at Michigan and his brief tenure at the University of Minnesota clearly were a transitional period for Dewey. In addition to writing lectures and teaching, he developed a greater understanding of the critical link between philosophy and education.

His research on the philosophy of experience, for example, helped shape his ideas on what is now known as experiential education, a core belief of his pedagogy. His ideas on the importance of building on the experiences of the child to achieve learning were a central curricular component of his famous lab school at the University of Chicago. Later he would develop his ideas on the importance of experience in his 1938 book *Experience and Education*.

In addition to this work, Dewey solidified his ideas on the importance of democracy at both the national level and in the classroom. In an early paper, for example, he wrote, "Democracy is the one, ultimate ethical ideal of humanity." Later Dewey developed his ideas on democratic education in his lab school and expanded them in his seminal *Democracy and Education*, published in 1916.

DEWEY IN CHICAGO

After a successful career at Michigan, Dewey was recruited to teach at the newly opened University of Chicago by then president William Rainey Harper. While Dewey was hesitant to move to the windy city, he was encouraged by his friend and colleague James Hayden Tufts who had joined the faculty of the new school in 1892.

Eventually Dewey made the 240-mile journey from Ann Arbor to Chicago for his interviews. He certainly must have been impressed with the magnificent World's Columbian Exposition that was in its full grandeur during his visit. Moreover, the promise of becoming the head of the Department of Philosophy sealed the deal.

His views on experimentalism also fit well with the ideas of two other distinguished members of the Department of Philosophy at the school, James Hayden Tufts and Herbert Mead. Dewey eagerly joined the faculty in the spring of 1894.

DEWEY MOVES TO CHICAGO

Dewey and his family moved into their temporary residence and within a year they settled into their permanent home near campus. They would remain in Chicago for the next decade.

Dewey's Chicago years were exciting, productive, but eventually disappointing. It was here that he established his famous lab school near the campus, began his prolific career as an author, and gained an international reputation. Nevertheless, he also received his share of criticism from more traditional educators and administrators.

THE LAB SCHOOL

The University of Chicago's Laboratory School, as it came to be known, was conceived and developed by John Dewey under the administrative direction of William Rainey Harper. Following months of preparation, the school opened its doors on January 13, 1896.

The school had a modest beginning with only twelve students and one teacher but had great promise as an educational experiment. It grew over the next year and its name was changed to the University Elementary School. By 1901 the school expanded to its peak enrollment of 140 students, 23 teachers, and 10 graduate student assistants.

The early years of the lab school represented a joyful experiment in learning. Its child-centered focus was innovative and refreshing. Dewey built his instructional framework on the interests of students and not the traditional curriculum at the time.

THE FOUR BASIC INTERESTS OF CHILDREN

Dewey contended that all children possessed four basic interests that represented the foundation of his lab school curriculum. These included communicating and discussing, making and building objects, exploring and investigating, and artistic expression.

Building on the ideas of Rousseau and Froebel, Dewey felt that learning must be based on the curiosity and experiences of students and not an abstract, prescribed, top-down curriculum. In short, students would learn naturally through real-life experiences.

Finally, Dewey applied his famous "learning by doing" principle with a "problem-solving" approach to education. He argued that children were enthusiastic about problem solving and with their innate curiosity and interest in investigating and exploring they would become engaged in learning.

PROBLEM SOLVING IN EDUCATION

As young students they might be presented with a problem of making bread or cookies and because of their interest in the subject would learn to read recipes, measure flour, and count eggs. As students matured, they would be introduced to more complex contemporary societal problems such as how to encourage a sense of community in an era of growing individualism.

While the teacher would introduce the problem, students typically worked in groups to develop solutions. Sometimes messy, sometimes a bit dreadful, these problem-solving exercises were the basis of learning at the lab school.

A JOYFUL EXPERIENCE

Not only was learning interesting, joyful, fun, and ultimately important and effective, teaching was much more rewarding in this new curricular environment. Dewey felt strongly that the teacher should not have to be a stern schoolmaster or disciplinarian who relied on corporal punishment, intimidation, testing, and grades.

Rather the classroom was conceived as an "embryonic democracy" in which teachers and students possessed a degree of intellectual freedom regarding the development of curriculum and instruction. Unlike more traditional classrooms of this period where the curriculum was dictated to teachers and students from above, the lab school was more democratic and it developed at the classroom level.

As a result, there were fewer administrative demands on the teachers in the lab school. This resulted in a greater autonomy and a more relaxed and less stressful environment. Engaged students were less likely to be disruptive or indifferent and therefore disciplinary problems were not the centerpiece of the teaching experience.

CHALLENGES OF THE LAB SCHOOL

But given the "experimental" nature of these classrooms there was a great deal of pushback from more traditional educators, administrators, and the general public. As a result, the "cacophony" of democratic classrooms gradually became a bit more constrained and the lab school gradually began to resemble more traditional classrooms.

General education teachers were gradually replaced with special subject teachers, classrooms became graded, and administrators gained more control.

THE SCHOOL'S FIRST "OUTLINE OF COURSE OF STUDY"

Then in 1898, under the supervision of Ella Flag Young (Dewey's former student), the school became even more traditional. The democratically structured curriculum at the classroom level was replaced by the school's first "Outline of Course of Study." As a result, student input into the development of the curriculum was diminished and their choices of projects were limited.

On the other hand, students were given the right to choose representatives to provide input to the administration and they also had the responsibility of maintaining discipline and order in the classroom.

TEACHERS, VISITORS, AND PARENTS CRITICIZE THE LAB SCHOOL

In addition to these administrative-based changes, teachers themselves began to recognize that the "problem solving" principle that was the centerpiece of the early curriculum was often taxing and difficult for students. Teachers found that sometimes they needed to use more traditional techniques of explanation and "top-down" learning so that students could understand the task at hand.

Finally, some visitors to the school were appalled by the apparent chaos that was typical of these early classrooms. Parents also criticized the school for not spending enough time teaching students reading, writing, and arithmetic. And yet these more "traditional" subjects were not the primary focus of the early classrooms.

Eventually, these criticisms would lead to further changes in the structure and curriculum of the school. While the lab school never abandoned its innovative focus, it did become more traditional over time.

THE CHILD AND THE CURRICULUM

Dewey learned a great deal from the early educational experiments at the lab school. In 1902, he summarized the ideas he derived from his work in *Child and the Curriculum*. In this important work, Dewey argued that there were two major schools of thought in education: the subject-centered and the child-centered.

Subject-centered learning employed a top-down approach in which the curriculum was developed by superintendents and administrators with some input from teachers themselves. Dewey felt that this traditional approach was flawed in that a student was considered a passive and a "superficial being who is to be deepened."

CRITIQUE OF SUBJECT-CENTERED LEARNING

This approach, moreover, did not allow democratic input from students and did not utilize their experiences to promote learning. For Dewey this form of learning was generally misdirected.

On the other hand, Dewey's experience at the lab school convinced him that the child-centered approach to education was flawed as well. The overemphasis on the role of the student often minimized the importance of the teacher and basic curricular content.

A SYNTHESIS OF SUBJECT AND CHILD-CENTERED EDUCATION

The solution, according to Dewey, was to synthesize these two educational approaches by presenting basic knowledge in a traditional format but also integrating the interests and experiences of students into the learning process. As Dewey noted, "the child and the curriculum are simply two limits which define a single process."

Nevertheless, Dewey warned educators that if traditional learning was not tempered with the child-centered approach, it could be dangerous. It would encourage passivity, stifle creativity and autonomy, and make students more compliant to authoritarianism.

DEWEY'S DEPARTURE FROM CHICAGO

Meanwhile Dewey's beloved lab school was experiencing some major administrative challenges. Even though it had reached its peak enrollment in 1901 and had the support of the community in general, there was a move to consolidate the school with Francis Parker's Chicago Institute.

The Chicago Institute was integrated into the University of Chicago system as the University Elementary School in 1902 under Dewey's leadership, but it experienced financial difficulties. Then in 1903, the two schools were formally consolidated and housed in the new Emmons Blaine Hall on the university campus.

INTERNAL TROUBLE AT THE LAB SCHOOL

Several problems immediately developed. Perhaps the most important of these was that the balance of power at the new school shifted. Many of the teachers from the former Chicago Institute (now representing 70 percent of the faculty) resented the leadership of Alice Chipman Dewey who had been appointed as principal of the school. There were accusations of her incompetence, though intraschool resentments and bickering certainly played a role as well.

Dewey attempted to resolve the situation but received little support from William Rainey Harper. Disgusted with the turmoil at the school, he resigned his position and with his family left the University of Chicago in 1904 for a new position at Columbia University. Thus a remarkable period in the history of education punctuated by the creation of the premier lab school in America had come to an end.

A NEW DIRECTION FOR THE LAB SCHOOL

With the departure of John Dewey and Alice Chipman, the new consolidated lab school dramatically changed course. Within just a few years, Charles Judd became the head of the school and remained there until 1938 when he retired.

Judd was a severe critic of Dewey and became a major advocate of eugenics as applied to education. His embrace of these views along with his support for the emerging standardized testing movement placed him at odds with Dewey's progressive approach to education.

TRAGEDY AND THE EARLY YEARS AT COLUMBIA

Before beginning his teaching duties at Columbia University, Dewey and his family traveled to Europe for a well-deserved vacation. But tragedy met them head on. Just weeks into their trip, their eight-year-old boy Gordon died in Ireland. Gordon had contracted typhoid fever on their ocean passage and passed away shortly after they arrived on the Emerald Isle.

This tragedy brought back horrific memories of their young son Morris who had contracted diphtheria and died in Milan in 1895.

THE DEWEYS MOURN

The Deweys buried their son and John returned to New York to begin his teaching duties. Distraught, Alice remained in Europe to resume her research. The family clearly was in mourning and both John and Alice were inconsolable.

John's first semester as a professor at Columbia was extremely difficult. He lived in a dormitory with students and was left to grieve alone in a strange new city. Finally, he negotiated released time from his teaching and in March 1905 he traveled to Italy to be with Alice and his four little girls. This reunion helped the family heal.

YOUNG SAVINO

The Deweys traveled to Venice and one evening while strolling through the piazza they noticed a young, handicapped, and emaciated boy. With his shinny dark hair, the boy reminded them of the two boys they had lost. When they returned from dinner, they brought him some food that he eagerly devoured.

The following day they returned to the piazza and once again engaged the young boy. John spoke with his mother and arranged for his "adoption." The poverty-stricken mother was happy that her young handicapped boy would now have a new life in the United States.

A NEW LIFE FOR THE DEWEYS

The Deweys soon returned to New York to begin a new life. Young Savino became a favorite among Alice, John, and the four Dewey girls.

In an age when eugenics was on the rise and handicapped children often were viewed with disdain, as products of inferior genetic makeup, the Deweys developed a greater sensitivity to those who were less fortunate. This would help shape the lives of the entire Dewey family.

COLUMBIA YEARS: TEACHER AND ACTIVIST

The years at Columbia University (1904–1930) were fruitful ones for John Dewey. He trained hundreds of students and was elected to numerous prominent positions in academia. He was an activist for labor, women's rights, and academic freedom.

He was a prolific author, traveled widely, and gave hundreds of academic presentations that spread the ideas of progressive education throughout the nation and the world. His vision of child-centered, experience-based, democratic education would be his enduring legacy.

In 1905, Dewey became the president of the American Philosophical Association and in 1916 a founding member of the American Federation of Teachers. Then in 1919, along with distinguished historians Charles Beard and James Harvey Robinson and economist Thorstein Veblen, he founded the influential New School for Social Research.

Dewey maintained his activism throughout his life. Early on he supported the rights of labor during the famous Pullman strike in 1894. It was in this context that he, his wife Alice, and Jane Addams vocally supported the workers' demands.

ACADEMIC FREEDOM

But it was academic freedom that remained the centerpiece of his activism. In 1915, these views took concrete expression when he and Arthur O. Lovejoy founded the American Association of University Professors (AAUP). This organization was created in response to the dismissal of numerous university professors throughout the nation because of their political views.

The AAUP promoted academic freedom for university and college professors with regard to the publication of research, classroom teaching, and, as citizens, the freedom to speak and write "free from institutional censorship." In addition, the organization advocated for academic tenure to protect these rights.

ACADEMIC PUBLICATIONS

Dewey's record of academic publication was astounding. All told he published more than seven hundred academic articles and forty books! During his years at Columbia he published a number of his most important books, including *Schools of To-Morrow* in 1915, a popular discussion of progressive schools throughout the United States.

The following year in 1916 he published his seminal work on progressive education titled *Democracy and Education* and then in 1925 he restated his basic principles regarding the importance of experience in education with his *Experience in Nature*.

TRAVEL: JAPAN, CHINA, THE SOVIET UNION, AND SOUTH AFRICA

Dewey continued to travel throughout the rest of his life. In 1919, he and Alice went to Japan while on sabbatical from Columbia. There he was invited to Peking University by two of his former students. Dewey remained in China for two years and gave over two hundred presentations promoting educational solutions to growing political problems in the region.

Then in the summer of 1928, a year after Alice passed away, Dewey and his daughter traveled to the Soviet Union to inspect both the political system of the nation and the schools that had been created. His *Impressions of Soviet Russia and the Revolutionary World* was published in 1929. His generally favorable, mostly balanced view of the USSR and its growing educational enterprise, however, was greeted with disdain by many Americans.

CONTROVERSY AFTER HIS SOVIET UNION TRIP

For example, Dewey noted that the schools in the USSR were clearly "the ideological arm of the revolution," but he was impressed with the number of schools that had been built since the revolution. In an age of Cold War, however, even the slightest recognition of any success in the Soviet Union was often seen as treasonous.

With the rise of Stalinism in the 1930s, Dewey's position on the Soviet Union changed. In his *Freedom and Culture*, published in 1939, he argued that the Soviet Union had essentially embraced age-old cultural tendencies, abandoned the ideals of Lenin and the revolution, and had moved toward authoritarianism.

SOUTH AFRICA

Following his controversial trip to the Soviet Union, John and his daughter Jane traveled to South Africa in July 1934 and attended the World Conference of New Education Fellowship in Cape Town and Johannesburg.

Dewey gave several talks on progressive education and collaboration and then traveled to Durban, Pretoria, and Victoria Falls, where he and Jane toured a number of schools and spoke to students and teachers. The trip was capped when he was given an honorary degree from the University of Witwatersrand.

LATER LIFE AND LEGACY

John spent the rest of his long life writing and lecturing in the United States. At the age of eighty-seven he married Roberta Grant, a New York heiress nearly half his age. The marriage was successful and the two lived happily in a spacious apartment in New York City until John's death in 1952.

John Dewey shook the world of education when he established his famous lab school at the University of Chicago in 1896. While his seminal ideas were far ahead of their time and difficult to implement, he set the course for child-centered democratic education in the United and the world.

Chapter Seven

W. E. B. Du Bois—Equality of African American Education

January 1, 1903

The sometimes quiet, sometimes violent struggle of African Americans to achieve racial justice in America reached a turning point at the beginning of the twentieth century.

THE PROMISE OF FREEDOM DEFERRED

The promise of freedom had been deferred as the country entered a vicious period of Jim Crow accompanied by a growing sense of the racial superiority of white Americans.

A central part of this struggle was education. Jim Crow America had determined that if black people were to receive even a modicum of education, it must be vocational. The primary argument, built around the pernicious philosophy of eugenics, was that African Americans were intellectually incapable of a classical education. Training for jobs in the modern industrial economy, however, made sense even among the most racist of Americans at that time.

But on January 1, 1903, W. E. B. Du Bois shook the world of education by demanding that black children be given the opportunity to receive a classical education rather than being tracked into "industrial" or vocational training.

Figure 7.1. W. E. B. Du Bois. Source: Library of Congress's Prints and Photographs Division.

THE SOULS OF BLACK FOLK

In his celebrated work *The Souls of Black Folk*, Du Bois challenged the racial stereotypes that were common in Jim Crow America. These stereotypes, he argued, were being reinforced by well-intentioned black educational endowments such as the Peabody/Slater Fund, the Rosenwald Fund, the Rockefeller Endowment, and the Jeanes Endowment. Moreover, Booker T. Washington, one of the most famous African American leaders at that time, also supported vocational training for African Americans.

This emerging consensus held that black people must learn a marketable skill in order to assimilate into white society. A classical education was rejected as being misguided and possibly dangerous. It was into this debate that W. E. B. Du Bois took a stand against what he saw as racist tracking of African Americans. He demanded that black people have equal access to a classical education.

EARLY LIFE

William Edward Burghardt Du Bois was born on February 23, 1868, in Great Barrington, Massachusetts. His mother, Mary Silvina Burghardt, was a free black and part of a small but closely knit black community. His father, Alfred Du Bois, had lived in Haiti most of his early life and then immigrated to the United States shortly before the American Civil War.

Mary and Alfred married on February 5, 1867, but he abandoned Mary and their infant son in 1870. Mary and William then returned to live with her parents in Great Barrington. When the young boy was only twelve years old, Mary suffered a major stroke and was bedridden for the next five years. She died in 1885.

WILLIAM'S PROTECTED ENVIRONMENT

Throughout these years William grew up under the watchful eye of his grandparents and extended family. He attended public schools and was one of just a few black people at the school. He played with white children and was generally accepted as part of the group.

William was a precocious child and his teachers encouraged him in his studies. He attended Searles High School in Great Barrington and like many of his classmates planned to go to college. His church, the First Congregational Church of Great Barrington, somehow raised the money for his tuition.

UNIVERSITY STUDY

With tuition money in his pocket but little else in the way of financial resources, William left Great Barrington in the fall of 1885 to attend Fisk University in Nashville, Tennessee. This was the first time that he had been in the South and it was here that he experienced racism firsthand.

Fisk was a historically black college situated in the heart of the Jim Crow South. William faced the reality of lynchings, disenfranchisement, and bigotry daily. The young boy who had grown up in the warm glow of a loving extended black family and a generally accepting white community now faced the challenges of a racist nation. He was changed forever.

HARVARD: A NEW START

William graduated from Fisk in 1888 and was accepted at Harvard College to continue his academic work. Although he was excited about the possibility of attending this premier institution, Harvard would not accept any of the credits that he had earned at Fisk. As a result, he would now begin his college career over again.

Nevertheless, he excelled at Harvard under the mentorship of his renowned professor William James. He paid his tuition and expenses by working summer jobs, he received a small inheritance, and he earned a scholarship. He completed his BA degree in history, cum laude, in two years, a remarkable feat for any student.

STUDIES AT BERLIN

William received another scholarship at Harvard to continue his graduate education in sociology, but in 1892 he was awarded a fellowship from the Slater Fund to attend the University of Berlin. He made the decision to go abroad. It was during his study at one of Europe's most prestigious institutions that William came of age.

While in Europe, he traveled widely, made many friends, and studied with some of the most influential scholars of the day including Gustav Schmoller and Heinrich von Treitschke.

Years later William reflected on his experience in Germany, noting that "I found myself on the outside of the American world, looking in. With me were white folk—students, acquaintances, teachers—who viewed the scene with me. They did not always pause to regard me as a curiosity . . . I was just a man."

Indeed, he was a man. He returned to Harvard and completed his doctoral degree in history, the first African American to do so! He was now ready to enter the working world as a highly regarded academic. Moreover, the seeds of his activism were sown.

EARLY ACADEMIC CAREER

Despite his impressive credentials, however, the doors of academia did not swing wide open for him. While his classmates from Harvard typically landed prestigious positions at top-rated schools, Du Bois felt lucky to get a job offer from Wilberforce College in Ohio.

He accepted the position and did quite well at this historically black school. Near the end of his tenure in 1886, he married Nina Gormer, one of his students.

The major turning point in his academic career, however, came during a short summer fellowship at the University of Pennsylvania. It was here that he began his field research in the black neighborhoods of Philadelphia. This work led to the first in-depth study of a black community. It was a monumental success.

THE PHILADELPHIA NEGRO

The result of his research, *The Philadelphia Negro*, published in 1899, was a critical reassessment of the negative stereotypes of African American communities in the United States.

His statistical, demographic analysis of the Philadelphia black community reaffirmed the problems in these neighborhoods, but Du Bois argued that the causes of poverty, crime, and illiteracy were not due to an inherent "social pathology" of black people but rather by racial discrimination as well as a lack of economic opportunities and education.

A NEW INTERPRETATION OF THE BLACK COMMUNITY

Du Bois concluded that black communities like those in Philadelphia possessed their own internal class structure and that all black people should not be judged on the basis of what he called the "submerged tenth." There was another group of black people (who he would later refer to as the "talented tenth") who also deserved attention and recognition.

The Philadelphia Negro was not only a major intellectual milestone for Du Bois's career, it also had a dramatic impact on his thinking about the "Negro Problem" in America. While he understood that only through racial integration would white America come to appreciate the talent and potential of the black community, he also argued that black people themselves must understand their unique heritage.

EMBRACING BLACK CULTURAL HISTORY

In short, African Americans should embrace their own history and culture while contributing to American society. This idea would be developed more fully in his *The Souls of Black Folks* published a few years later.

In many ways this was the basis of his lifelong approach to African American education. Black people should not be tracked into vocational occupations. They should be given the opportunity to receive a classical education, achieve personal growth, and contribute to the wider society.

BOOKER T. WASHINGTON

As Du Bois completed his manuscript in 1897, he accepted a position at another historically black institution, Atlanta University. Here as professor of economics and history he taught, conducted research, and wrote extensively. He was also confronted with a powerful message delivered by Booker T. Washington.

In fact, it is no exaggeration that the reaction to Booker T. Washington's Atlanta Compromise Speech of 1895 and his classic work *Up from Slavery* published six years later would become the catalyst for the modern civil rights movement.

UP FROM SLAVERY

Up from Slavery, published in 1901, reflected Washington's vision of African American education. A classical education, he maintained, would simply give black children promises that could not be fulfilled.

He made this point by referencing a hypothetical young black man who had just graduated from high school who, "sitting down in a one room cabin with grease on his clothing, filth all around him and weeds in the yard and garden, engaged in studying French grammar." This image resonated with the white community but outraged many African Americans at the time.

Washington's idea was simple: in a society built on slavery and racial segregation African Americans must work hard and receive some form of vocational training. Years earlier, in 1881, Washington had founded the successful Tuskegee Institute whose primary mission was to train black teachers to help students build self-reliance and develop skills in a practical trade.

ATLANTA COMPROMISE SPEECH

But Washington's most powerful statement on vocation/industrial training for African Americans was his Atlanta Compromise Speech in 1895. This famous speech launched what has been called the Atlanta Compromise, a tacit agreement that black people would acquiesce to white rule and tolerate segregation and discrimination in return for free vocational education.

The Atlanta Compromise Speech was delivered on September 18, 1895, to the Cotton States and International Exposition. Speaking before a white audience, Washington assured Southern leaders that African Americans were ready and able to help them develop a prosperous economy and a peaceful society.

CAST DOWN YOUR BUCKETS

Washington's famous statement "Cast down your bucket where you are" resonated with the audience. He reassured white planters and industrialists alike that black people "without strikes and labor wars, [those who had] tilled your fields, cleared your forests, built your railroads and cities and brought forth treasures . . . from the earth" were ready to help the South prosper again.

And with a nod to the importance of vocational education he noted that the "greatest danger [for African Americans] . . . in the great leap from slavery to freedom" was that they "may overlook the fact that they shall prosper . . . as [they] learn to dignify and glorify common labor, and put brains and skill into the common occupations of life."

RESENTMENT IN THE BLACK COMMUNITY

Washington concluded by saying, "No race can prosper until it learns that there is as much dignity in tilling a field as in writing a poem. It is at the bottom of life we must begin and not at the top. Nor should we permit our grievances to overshadow our opportunities."

While his words made perfect sense to the white audience in Atlanta that September day, there was a growing resentment to them among early African American civil rights leaders, including W. E. B. Du Bois.

DU BOIS CHALLENGES WASHINGTON

W. E. B. Du Bois was not opposed to vocational training for some African Americans in the racist Jim Crow era, but he also favored access to a classical education, especially for the "talented tenth" of the black population.

Moreover, he was not content with the "scraps of education" that were given to the black community through well-intentioned philanthropic groups, nor with the idea promoted by Booker T. Washington that black education should be consigned exclusively to vocational and industrial training.

EQUAL EDUCATIONAL OPPORTUNITIES

In the burning fires of Jim Crow, Du Bois demanded that African American children be given the same educational opportunities as white children. This idea not only challenged the prevailing mindset of liberal white America, but it also brought the issue of education firmly into the modern civil rights movement that was emerging during this period.

In his classic work *The Souls of Black Folk*, published in 1903, Du Bois leveled searing criticism of Washington's Atlanta Compromise "gospel of work and money." He called this idea a thinly veiled attempt to curry favor with his wealthy white supporters (of Tuskegee) and went on to call Washington "the most distinguished southerner since Jefferson Davis, "the president of the Confederate States of America."

THE IMPORTANCE OF *THE SOULS OF BLACK FOLK*

The Souls of Black Folk was so important that the great civil rights activist James Weldon Johnson once noted that its impact was comparable to that of *Uncle Tom's Cabin*.

In *The Souls of Black Folk*, Du Bois reiterated his famous dictum first developed in *The Philadelphia Negro*: the "problem of the twentieth century was the problem of the color line." The two overarching themes of this work were the cultural parity between black people and white people and the double consciousness that was developing among African Americans during the difficult period of Jim Crow.

NEITHER ASSIMILATION NOR SEPARATISM

Du Bois argued that this double consciousness would help sustain African Americans in the future as they contributed to white American culture, on the one hand, and embraced their own identity. As Du Bois wrote, "the destiny of the race [would lead] neither to assimilation nor separatism but to proud, enduring hyphenation."

But his criticism of Booker T. Washington's vision of education was the central feature of this important book. In chapter 3 (of fourteen chapters), titled "On Mr. Booker T. Washington and Others," he rejected Washington's plea to white America to "throw down your buckets" to the black community and that African Americans would help rebuild the South. In return, black people would receive free "industrial" education.

He noted that "Mr. Washington's cult" had gained many followers—both black and white—and that "one hesitates, therefore, to criticize a life which, beginning with so little, [had] done so much." And yet the time had come for such criticism!

DU BOIS'S SEARING CRITICISM OF WASHINGTON

Du Bois argued forcefully that despite Washington's growing success and popularity he represented "the old attitude of adjustment and submission" for black people. He wrote that Washington had asked that African Americans give up three things: political power, insistence on civil rights, and higher education of "Negro youth."

He noted, moreover, that Washington's ideas, expressed in the Atlanta Compromise Speech of 1895, had not worked. In fact, things had gotten much worse for African American people. In the years since this speech, black Americans had been disenfranchised, their legal status degraded to that of "civil inferiority," and there had been a "steady withdrawal of aid from institutions for the higher training of the Negro."

DU BOIS REJECTS "APOLOGIES FOR INJUSTICE"

Du Bois concluded by saying that African Americans will gladly follow Washington's ideas of personal thrift and self-help. On the other hand, they must reject his "apologies for injustice," that ignores the privilege and duty of voting, promotes caste distinctions, and "opposes the higher training and ambition of our brighter minds."

Du Bois's stance on black education positioned him not only as the vanguard of the early civil rights movement but also situated education in the forefront of the struggle for racial equality.

DU BOIS'S GLOBAL ACTIVISM

His struggle, however, was not confined to the United States—it was global. This was evident when, in the summer of 1900, Du Bois attended the first Pan African Conference, held in London. Here he helped draft the famous "Address to the Nations of the World" that appealed to European leaders to abandon their imperial ambitions, allow self-governance in their colonies, and permit individual rights to people of color throughout the world.

In addition, the "Address" implored leaders of the United States to "protect the rights of people of African descent," a recognition of the growing problem of racism during the height of the Jim Crow era.

"THE PROBLEM OF THE TWENTIETH CENTURY IS THE PROBLEM OF THE COLOR LINE"

The address was signed by international leaders of the African freedom movement along with W. E. B. Du Bois as chairman of the Committee on the Address. In a sentence that would resonate for decades to come, Du Bois once again declared his famous dictum: "The problem of the twentieth century is the problem of the color line."

Du Bois clearly had begun to challenge racial discrimination in the United States and throughout the world. His work on *The Philadelphia Negro*, his participation in the First Pan African Conference, and his celebrated work *The Souls of Black Folk* demonstrated that the ultimate solution to "the problem of the twentieth century" was education.

NIAGARA MOVEMENT

But while Du Bois was keenly interested in the problem of global racism, discrimination, and colonialism, it was the growing menace of Jim Crow America that was his primary concern and the focus of his early activism. In 1905, he and several important figures in the civil rights struggle including Fredrick McGhee and Jesse Max Barber traveled to the Canadian side of Niagara Falls to discuss problems of racial discrimination.

The conference was held in Canada and not the United States as a symbolic gesture protesting the escalating racism in the United States. The group prepared a declaration of principles and officially incorporated the Niagara Movement in 1906.

"TWO CLASSES OF NEGROES"

Still stinging from the Atlanta Compromise Speech of Booker T. Washington over a decade before, Reverdy C. Ransom summarized the position of the Niagarites in their second conference in 1906. With reference to Washington, Ransom noted, "Today, two classes of Negroes . . . are standing at the parting of the ways. The one counsels patient submission to our present humiliations . . . [the other] does not believe in bartering its manhood for the sake of gain."

Although support for Washington's accommodationist position would continue for some time, the toxic mix of discrimination, disenfranchisement, and lynching during this period slowly began to shift support toward the position of Du Bois and the Niagarites.

ACADEMIC ACTIVISM

But it was in 1909 when Du Bois presented his important paper "Reconstruction and Its Benefits" to the American Historical Association that his crusading efforts on behalf of African Americans reached a wider academic audience.

Du Bois was the first African American to be invited to the prestigious conference and his paper was a bombshell. He argued forcefully against the prevailing interpretation of Reconstruction as a failure due to the incompetence and indolence of black people.

CHALLENGING THE "DUNNING SCHOOL"

Scholars of the so-called Dunning School from Columbia had argued for years that black people themselves had destroyed any chance for a successful Reconstruction of the nation following the Civil War because they were not ready for citizenship, much less positions of political leadership.

Du Bois challenged that notion by arguing that the brief period of the early 1870s, when black people gained the right to vote and elected a number of African Americans to political office, was actually very successful. During this period, democracy was expanded, public schools thrived under the Freedmen's Bureau, and numerous land disputes were settled by Bureau courts.

THE REAL FAILURE OF RECONSTRUCTION

For Du Bois, the real failure of Reconstruction was that the federal government essentially had abandoned their support for African Americans after 1877, forcing them to fare for themselves against the growing power of a white-dominated South.

Although the paper was generally ignored by most historians at the time, Du Bois expanded his ideas into a book, *Reconstruction*, in 1935. This book paved the way for a more balanced vision of Reconstruction in general and, more specifically, a better understanding of the role of African Americans during this period. Today his interpretation is widely accepted as the standard by most historians across the nation.

NAACP—CIVIL RIGHTS AND EDUCATION

Just a few months before Du Bois delivered his important paper on Reconstruction to the American Historical Association, he attended the National Negro Conference in New York. The meeting led to the establishment of the National Negro Committee and the following year the National Association for the Advancement of Colored People (NAACP).

Du Bois was the driving force behind the creation of this important organization. His standing in the academic community, his leadership among early African American civil rights figures, his work on the problem of international racism and colonialism, and his important stand on the equality of opportunity in education for African Americans placed him at the forefront of this group.

EDITOR OF *THE CRISIS*

Du Bois essentially shaped the direction of the NAACP as its director of publicity and research. Perhaps more important, he was the editor of *The Crisis*, the powerful publication of the group, for many years.

The NAACP became a major advocate of equal education for African Americans and with its Legal Defense Fund fought in the courts to achieve racial justice. The long struggle for the desegregation of public education essentially began during this period, reaching its crescendo in 1954 with the famous *Brown v. Board of Education* Supreme Court decision.

The Crisis was a huge success. By 1920 it had a circulation of over one hundred thousand. Throughout these years, moreover, *The Crisis* supported racial justice, equal educational opportunities for African Americans, women's rights, union rights, and even interracial marriage.

LATER LIFE AND ACTIVISM

Although there often was tension between Du Bois and the leadership of the NAACP, he remained at the helm of *The Crisis* until 1933 when he was removed as editor. The following year he returned to Atlanta University and became the chair of the Department of Sociology. It was here that he continued his prodigious publication record, writing numerous books and articles for the cause of racial justice.

CRITIC OF U.S. FOREIGN POLICY

During this period, Du Bois also became a vocal critic of the U.S. government. He opposed America's entry into World War II and especially its use of nuclear weapons on Japan in 1945.

During the Cold War of the late 1940s and early 1950s, his opposition to nuclear proliferation became an important part of his social and political activism. In 1950, he was one of the founding members of the Peace Information Center (PIC) that promoted an international ban on nuclear weapons.

AGENT OF A FOREIGN STATE?

The U.S. Department of Justice, however, perceived the PIC as an "agent of a foreign state" and as such required that its leadership register with the federal government. As a symbolic gesture, Du Bois and others refused and were indicted.

Du Bois was tried by the Justice Department in 1951 but was not convicted. The case was quickly dismissed when his defense attorney informed the judge that Albert Einstein had agreed to testify as a character witness for Du Bois!

SHUNNED AND CELEBRATED

Although he was not convicted of a crime, the federal government confiscated his passport for eight years. Moreover, Du Bois lost the support of many civil rights groups including the NAACP. On the other hand, he became a sort of cult hero among leftist organizations and unions throughout the country.

Du Bois continued his advocacy for world peace, disarmament, and racial justice for the next eight years until his passport was released to him. In 1958, Du Bois and his wife, Shirley Graham, embarked on a world tour visiting the Soviet Union and the People's Republic of China. Then in 1960, he was invited by President Kwame Nkrumah to celebrate the establishment of the Republic of Ghana. Du Bois and Nkrumah got along very well, and they discussed the possibility of publishing a massive *Encyclopedia of Africana*.

THE GREAT MAN PASSES

The following year, in October 1961, Du Bois returned to Ghana to begin the project. Then in early 1963, the U.S. government once again refused to renew his passport. As a symbolic gesture of protest, he became a citizen of Ghana, though he did not renounce his U.S. citizenship.

A few months later, on August 27, 1963, the great man passed from this earth at the age of ninety-five and was buried with honors in Ghana. In the United States his passing did not go unnoticed. On August 28, 1963, during the famous March on Washington, Roy Wilkins, executive secretary of the NAACP, called for a moment of silence to honor the important legacy of this great man.

Du Bois was a pioneer civil rights advocate, supported a broad range of reforms, advocated for an end to colonialization, promoted nuclear disarmament, and he shook the world of education when, on January 1, 1903, he challenged the prevailing vision of African American education and demanded equal opportunities for all children—both black and white. His legacy will endure.

Chapter Eight

Horace Mann Bond—A Challenge to Standardized Testing

March 1, 1924

America in the 1920s has been perceived as an exciting period when our economy boomed, flappers danced the Charleston, and speakeasies dotted the urban landscape.

A DARKER SIDE OF THE ROARING TWENTIES

But beyond the excitement and cultural changes was a darker reality. World War I had left a deep scar on our collective psyche and elements of anti-Semitism, xenophobia, and racism advanced in its wake. The KKK grew in numbers and spread from pockets of the South to engulf much of the North as well. And equally as troubling, American had isolated itself from the world and it embraced a new anti-immigrant mentality.

During this difficult time, Congress passed a series of new immigration laws collectively known as the National Origins Acts. These laws essentially restricted the entry of southeastern Europeans, Jews, and Asian and Latin American people.

THE PLAGUE OF EUGENICS

At the heart of this new pernicious mentality was eugenics, a dangerous pseudo-science that promoted the ideas of social Darwinism. Eugenicists argued that people from more "advanced" nations (meaning white people)

Figure 8.1. Horace Mann Bond. Source: Wikipedia, public domain photographs.

were "superior" to others. Moreover, new "standardized" intelligence tests appeared to provide positive scientific evidence "proving" these eugenicist claims.

THE EMERGENCE OF STANDARDIZED TESTING

But then on June 8, 1924, Horace Mann Bond shook the world of education by challenging the inherent biased interpretations of standardized test results. His action set the course for a rejection of the racist hereditarianism argument regarding the intellectual inferiority of both African Americans and immigrants.

When Horace Mann Bond took his stand against standardized testing, he faced a powerful juggernaut. By the early 1920s, standardized testing had made its way into the schools of America, and there was a frenzy of acceptance by school superintendents, administrators, and some teachers.

THE ROOTS OF STANDARDIZED TESTING

The roots of this movement can be traced directly to the last decades of the nineteenth century when Sir Francis Galton published his research on heredity. Galton pioneered our understanding differences in individuals, including intelligence. But his research also opened the door to the disturbing pseudo-science of eugenics.

SOCIAL DARWINISM

Eugenics was the dangerous belief that certain races were inherently inferior to others. It was built around the idea of "social Darwinism" that had perverted Charles Darwin's metaphorical notion of "survival of the fittest" in the evolution of new species of plant and animal life.

G. STANLEY HALL

By the late nineteenth century, eugenics had made its way into the scientific study of psychology and was promoted by scholars such as G. Stanley Hall and many others. As the founder of the *American Journal of Psychology* and the first president of the American Psychological Association (APA), Hall commanded great respect.

Like other eugenicists of the day, Hall had disdain for what he called "defectives." These included the intellectually weak, the mentally ill, the sick, the poor, immigrants, and African Americans. Along with Galton and others, he favored selective breeding of those with superior intelligence as well as sterilization of "imperfect" individuals.

As president of Clark University for many years, Hall mentored dozens of PhDs in psychology who went on to spread the ideas of eugenics. These included such towering figures as Lewis Terman, James Cattell, Henry Goddard, Edmund Sanford, and John Dewey, who, as we have seen, broke with Hall over the validity of eugenics.

ALFRED BINET: TESTING AS DIAGNOSTIC

About the same time, Alfred Binet began his studies at the Sorbonne in Paris. It was here that he was influenced by the work of Francis Galton, Hall, and others and developed an instrument to determine mental differences among individuals. His work caught the attention of the French Ministry of Public Instruction and Binet was commissioned to help identify learning disabled children.

Binet's research yielded his classic *Experimental Studies in Intelligence,* published in 1903. This work was written to develop a methodology to distinguish between "the normal child and the abnormal." The foundation of mental testing had now been established.

BINET-SIMON SCALE

Two years later, Binet and his student Theodore Simon developed their Binet-Simon scale—the world's first intelligence test. Binet and Simon continued their research and by 1908 they had created a series of tests that they felt were appropriate for students from age three to thirteen.

But while Binet and Simon had developed their examination to diagnose mental problems for remediation, others had a darker use for them. Henry Goddard, yet another student of G. Stanley Hall, was one of those who used mental testing not as a diagnostic tool but simply as an instrument to sort individuals and promote his vision of eugenics.

GODDARD: FATHER OF INTELLIGENCE TESTING

Goddard was the early lynchpin between mental testing and eugenics and is often referred to as the "father of intelligence testing." As the director of research at the Vinland Training School for Feebleminded Boys and Girls, Goddard translated Binet and Simon's work into English and set out to prove the racial superiority of the "white race."

He distributed twenty-two thousand copies of the translated Binet-Simon scale to schools throughout the nation. While widespread testing did not catch on at this time, Goddard had opened the door further to the use of standardized examinations in schools.

THE KALLIKAK FAMILY AND THE "IQ"

Goddard soon established himself as an important figure in mental testing with the publication of *The Kallikak Family: A Study in the Heredity of Feeblemindedness* in 1912. It was here that he introduced the concept of the intelligence quotient (IQ) as well as the standard nomenclature of individuals with low IQs including morons, imbeciles, and idiots. Goddard actually coined the now pejorative term *moron* in that study.

GODDARD'S ELLIS ISLAND'S TESTING

Goddard then went on to create a testing program at Ellis Island to establish the validity of his IQ test. He selected a sample of immigrants who had previously been classified as "feebleminded" and administered his test to them. The exam, as expected, accurately predicted their "mental status," and he used this finding to declare a major victory for standardized testing.

Four years later in 1916, Goddard published an article in the *Journal of Delinquency* titled "Mental Tests and the Immigrant." This article summarized his finding from the Ellis Island tests and provided a clear link between his work in testing and his theories on eugenics.

He proudly noted that the use of his mental examinations had led to a dramatic increase in the number of deportations based on feeblemindedness. He boasted that "the number of aliens deported . . . increased approximately 350 percent in 1913 and 570 percent in 1914."

STANFORD-BINET EXAM

While Goddard had sought to validate both mental testing and his darker ideas regarding eugenics, it was another student of G. Stanley Hall, Lewis Terman, who improved the Binet-Simon scale with his "Stanford Revision" of the test.

This test, now commonly known as the Stanford-Binet Exam, was designed to classify children who were developmentally disabled. It was eagerly embraced by psychologists and educators alike at the time and is now in its fifth revision.

EUGENICS—AN IMPORTANT COMPONENT OF TESTING

Later Terman would develop tests for non-English speakers, Native Americans, Mexicans, and "unschooled" African Americans. This testing led him to write that the inherent dullness of these individuals was "racial or at least inherent in the family stocks from which they came." He went on to conclude that "from a eugenics point of view they constitute a grave problem, because of their unusually prolific breeding."

REMEDIATION VERSUS SORTING

Thus by the eve of World War 1, the focus of standardized testing had changed fundamentally. What was once designed as an instrument to identify individuals with mental problems or learning disabilities and then help to provide remediation for those conditions had become an instrument of sorting individuals.

While Alfred Binet, Theodore Simon, and others had used their standardized exams to understand learning problems and intervene to help them deal with or solve those conditions, individuals such as Henry Goddard, Lewis Terman, and other eugenicists used these exams to "scientifically prove" the superiority of the "white race."

WORLD WAR I AND TESTING

The fundamental shift in the vision of standardized exams from diagnosis and remediation to sorting and classification came during World War 1.

The United States was a latecomer to the conflict that began in Europe in 1914. However, when it entered the war in the spring of 1917, the U.S. initiated a massive recruitment, enlistment, and conscription effort to raise an army to join allies in Europe.

By the end of the war, the United States had registered over 9.5 million men for the draft, with nearly three million inducted into the army. Another million men either enlisted or were drawn from the ranks of the National Guard. Two million men eventually went to Europe.

ROBERT YERKES AND THE ALPHA TEST

Because of the enormous numbers of men who suddenly were part of the military, some argued that an examination-based classification system was needed to direct individuals to different occupations within the service. Among those advocating for such a program was Robert M. Yerkes, then president of the APA.

Yerkes saw the possibility of large-scale mental testing in the army as an important step in promoting standardized testing throughout the nation. For him, this also was a golden opportunity for the emerging field of psychometrics.

Yerkes initiated a vigorous campaign to convince the leadership of the U.S. military that these tests would be useful, noting that they would "increase the efficiency of the Army and Navy" by identifying mentally incompetent recruits. He then organized several committees within the APA to examine the usefulness of these tests and then chaired the powerful Psychological Examination of Recruits Committee.

TESTING BEGINS

By the summer of 1917, this committee had completed its work and under the direction of Yerkes submitted a proposal to the military command. Although there was a degree of initial skepticism among military leaders, Yerkes was given a commission in the army as a major and testing began.

Yerkes recruited forty young psychologists from universities and private practice to conduct the testing program. Each was commissioned in the army under the Sanitary Corps. By the fall of 1917, over eighty thousand recruits had been tested. This early success gave credibility to the program and the War College approved further testing.

The Alpha test, as it was called, was based on the Stanford-Binet model and later a Beta exam was developed for "illiterates." By May 1918, the Sanitary Corps had tested over two hundred thousand "doughboys" each month. And yet a vast number of recruits had not been tested.

GENERAL ORDER NO. 74

In August 1918, General "Blackjack" Pershing, commanding general of the U.S. Army, became convinced of the need for more testing, and he issued General Order No. 74. This order dramatically expanded the testing program, and standardized testing was now given full support by the U.S. military.

When the war ended in November 1918, the Alpha and Beta testing program was abandoned, but its apparent success and its support from the military leadership gave standardized testing enormous credibility.

A NEW ERA OF TESTING

Soon testing would become commonplace in businesses and schools throughout America. Moreover, the "success" of these and other standardized tests provided the basis of support for the Emergency Quota Act of 1921 and later the immigration restriction laws of 1922 and 1924, commonly known as the National Origin Acts.

THE ALPHA TEST AND PUBLIC EDUCATION

The army Alpha and Beta tests had a dramatic effect on education policy and assessment. First, they demonstrated the pathetic level of literacy in the nation, with nearly one-third of all recruits classified as illiterate.

Second, the level of educational attainment was disturbing. Over half of the native-born white recruits tested had less than seven total years of education, while immigrants had just over four and a half years. African

Americans, on the other hand, had an average of two and one-half years of education!

THE GREAT PROMISE OF TESTING

Perhaps more importantly for educators was that these tests promised to be an effective, scientific assessment of individuals to determine their mental abilities. Even before the Alpha and Beta tests were completed, school officials from all over the country had written to Yerkes requesting information on the tests and how they could be used in the classroom.

THE NATIONAL ACHIEVEMENT TEST

Building on the excitement over the use of standardized tests in schools, the General Education Board of the Rockefeller Foundation provided an enormous grant of $25,000 to the National Research Council to develop tests similar to the Alpha exams that could be used in schools.

The National Research Council appointed a committee headed by Yerkes to develop such an exam and by the early spring of 1919, they had produced a test and distributed two hundred thousand copies of it to schools across America.

PUBLIC EXCITEMENT OVER TESTING

These early "National Achievement Tests" were administered and reconfigured over the next few months, and by 1921 they had sold over a half million of these exams to schools. There seemed to be no end to the demand for national achievement tests, and by 1923 millions of them had been administered to students. The standardized test had captured the imagination of educators throughout the country and we would never be the same.

HORACE MANN BOND CHALLENGES STANDARDIZED TESTING

It was in this frenzied environment that a young Horace Mann Bond took his stand. While most educators—administrators and teachers—blindly accepted the validity of the multiple choice, standardized exam, a small group of educators and civil rights activists took a very unpopular position. They questioned the foundation of the exams themselves and argued that interpretations of their results were biased.

Horace Mann Bond shook the world of education on March 1, 1924, when he published his article "Intelligence Testing and Propaganda" in the NAACP's official publication *The Crisis*.

CARL BRIGHAM: *A STUDY OF AMERICAN INTELLIGENCE*

This pathbreaking article was written as a challenge to a recently published book by Carl Brigham, one of the young psychologists who had administered the Alpha tests during World War I. Brigham's book *A Study of American Intelligence* claimed to scientifically explain the differences in mental abilities of groups of Americans.

Brigham's work was a sensation. It built on the growing acceptance of standardized testing, on the one hand, and the dark philosophy of eugenics, on the other.

BRIGHAM'S FINDINGS

Brigham had three major findings. The first was that "of all the racial groups, negroes had the lowest intelligence." Second, he noted that black people in the Northern states had higher intelligence scores than those in the South. And finally, he wrote that northern Europeans had higher intelligence scores than white people from southern Europe.

In short, Brigham reinforced the prevailing eugenics arguments of the day by indicating that both African Americans and immigrants were intellectually inferior.

HORACE MANN BOND'S CHALLENGE

While the majority of the nation's intellectuals (and sadly educators) accepted these findings as scientific fact, Horace Mann Bond rejected them out of hand. He wrote that Brigham's claims were being used as propaganda to justify reduced funding for black schools.

In addition, Bond tacitly rejected the eugenics argument of the intellectual inferiority of immigrants. As we have seen, it was during this period that the nation had turned its back on immigration. Congress passed a series of National Origins Acts that dramatically limited immigration to this nation.

In short, Horace Mann Bond at the age of nineteen had not only challenged the effectiveness and scientific basis of standardized testing but also the egregious notions of eugenics that had swept through the nation at this time.

HORACE MANN BOND: EARLY YEARS

Horace Mann Bond was born into a middle-class family in Nashville, Tennessee, on November 8, 1904. He was the sixth of seven children to James and Jane Bond. Both his maternal and paternal grandparents had grown up in the shadow of slavery.

Horace's father, James, was the illegitimate son of Jane Crockett Arthur, a slave who had been given to Preston and Belinda Bond as a wedding present. Preston fathered James, and the entire family—both white and black—lived in the same household. As a result, James was exposed to books, music, and deeply held religious convictions.

H. M. BOND'S PARENTS

By all accounts James was a precocious child and attended local schools in the area. Later he was accepted at Oberlin College where he studied for the ministry, eventually earning his doctorate in theology.

While at Oberlin he met Jane Alice Brown who was studying to become a teacher. The couple married on Christmas Eve 1895. Nine years later, James and Jane Bond had a son who they named after the great educator Horace Mann.

YOUNG HORACE

Young Horace thus grew up in a household of educated parents and benefited from the teachings of his mother and the religious training of his father. In addition, he was instilled with a sense of social justice from both parents, values that he would hold throughout his life.

Like his father James Bond (yes, James Bond), Horace was a precocious child and graduated from high school at the age of fourteen. He then went on to Lincoln University where he earned his BA in history at the age of nineteen.

HORACE AT THE UNIVERSITY OF CHICAGO

Horace then enrolled at the University of Chicago where he earned his master's degree in 1926 and his doctorate in 1936. It was during his time at the University of Chicago that he wrote his extraordinary article (at the age of nineteen) that challenged the use of standardized exams both as an assessment of mental ability and as an excuse for the perverted notions of eugenics.

This article propelled the young man into the civil rights community, and he received special recognition from the editor of *The Crisis*, W. E. B. Du Bois.

EARLY TEACHING ASSIGNMENTS

While Horace was working on his doctorate at the University of Chicago, he taught and did administrative work at several historically black schools. One of his early teaching assignments was at Langston University in Langston, Oklahoma, in 1934. It was here that he developed his skills of pragmatic political accommodation even though he was committed to W. E. B. Du Bois's idea of equality of educational opportunities for African Americans.

HORACE AND "PICKIN' PEAS"

When state legislators visited Langston University to consider reduced funding for the school, Horace wined and dined the delegation. He helped arrange a glorious banquet for the group and served them fried chicken. The group was then entertained with a play performed by university students, the theme of which was field hands "pickin' peas."

Through these actions, Horace managed to convince the somewhat skeptical group of legislators that the school was not a threat to the white population of Oklahoma. Rather Langston University was introducing black students to vocational, domestic sciences and "honest labor and toil." The school received full funding for the next academic year.

ACADEMIC ADMINISTRATION

After several years at Langston, Horace was offered a deanship at Dillard University in New Orleans. He then went on to chair the Department of Education at Fisk University. While teaching at Fisk, Horace met and married Julia Agnes Washington in 1929. The couple had three children including Julian Bond in 1940. Julian would carry on the tradition of his parents' activism to become a leader of the Student Nonviolent Coordinating Committee in the 1960s. Later he became the chairman of the NAACP for over a decade, from 1998 to 2010.

In 1939, Horace became the first president of the Fort Valley State College in Fort Valley, Georgia. He remained at the school for six years until 1945. During this period, he expanded the school's curriculum, transformed it into a four-year institution, and doubled its capital base.

PRESIDENT OF LINCOLN UNIVERSITY

His success at Dillard University, Fisk University, and Fort Valley State University led to his appointment as the first black president of Lincoln University. Horace led the school for twelve years until 1957 when he accepted a position as dean of education at Atlanta University (now Clark-Atlanta University). Horace remained there until 1972, when he passed.

RESEARCH AND WRITING

Throughout his distinguished career as a teacher and administrator at historically black institutions, Horace Mann Bond continued his research, writing, and activism. He completed his dissertation in 1936 under the direction of such notable scholars as Newton Edwards, longtime editor of the *Elementary School Journal*; Frank S. Freeman, specialist in testing and measurement; and the great Robert Park in urban sociology.

In 1934, he published an education text for black colleges titled *The Education of the Negro in the American Social Order*. Then five years later, in 1939, he published his classic *Negro Education in Alabama: A Study in Cotton and Steel* based on his dissertation research.

THE 1924 *CRISIS* ARTICLE

This early work on African American education as well as his leadership at historically black colleges provided the foundation of his unrelenting critique of intelligence testing beginning with his article in *The Crisis* in 1924. This was followed by another scathing review of intelligence testing titled "What the Army Intelligence Tests Measured" published in July 1924 in *Opportunity*, the journal of the National Urban League.

His opening sentence in *The Crisis* article gives us a sense of the anger, frustration, and outrage that young Horace Mann Bond had for standardized testing and the inherent bias of these tests. He wrote that "it has ever been the bane of any development in science that its results in the hands [of] . . . biased observers may be twisted to [become] weapons for the prejudiced."

PUBLICATION IN *OPPORTUNITY*

In his second article published in *Opportunity* the following month, Bond eviscerated the findings of Brigham and others, noting that "all tests so far devised . . . and all so called racial differences identified can be resolved into social differences." In short, it was the environment of racism in the United

States and not the presumed inherent intellectual inferiority of African Americans that accounted for variations in test scores.

REJECTION OF GENETIC/RACIAL INTERPRETATION OF TEST SCORES

Bond noted that African Americans' test scores from some Northern states were higher than white peoples' from a number of Southern states. This of course contradicted the basic genetic/racial interpretation of test score differences. In addition, he demonstrated that while test scores were higher in Northern states and thus were seen by some as evidence of the superiority of the "Nordic race," Bond pointed out that there were many southern and eastern Europeans included in the Northern sample.

TESTING AS A DIAGNOSTIC INSTRUMENT

Although Bond was critical of Brigham's work as well as other racist and eugenic interpretations of the army Alpha test data, he did see a use for these types of exams as diagnostic instruments. Like other test developers, then and now, Bond rejected standardized intelligence and achievement exams used to sort and discriminate against certain groups.

Three years after the publication of his pathbreaking article in *The Crisis*, he published another piece in that same journal titled "Some Exceptional Negro Children." This work was based on his research and testing of thirty black elementary students from Chicago schools. He showed that nearly two-thirds of the group scored above 106 on the Stanford-Binet test, while over a quarter of them scored more than 130, a level attained by about 1 percent of all test takers.

BOND'S SUPPORT OF THE ENVIRONMENTALIST POSITION

More important, Bond argued that exposure to reading material in the home as well as parental encouragement and intellectual stimulation accounted for most of the variation in test scores. This interpretation, of course, has been replicated over the years by numerous educational researchers.

Although the acceptance of standardized testing continued to grow during these years, Bond had helped to open the door to what has been called an environmentalist interpretation of test results.

SLOW RETREAT OF THE EUGENICS INTERPRETATION

Gradually the strictly hereditarian or eugenic argument lost a great deal of its initial support. In fact, by 1930, Carl Brigham recanted much of his earlier eugenic interpretations of the army Alpha test data in his article "Intelligence Tests and Immigrant Groups" in *Psychological Review*.

During the difficult economic times of the 1930s, Bond wrote little on standardized testing, focusing instead on his administrative duties at Dillard, Fisk, and Fort Valley State College. And although he did not publish in the area of testing, it is clear that he maintained his critique of biased interpretations of testing results.

BOND'S ROLE IN THE *BROWN V. BOARD OF EDUCATION* DECISION

When Bond returned to his alma mater as president of Lincoln University in 1945, however, his activism was once again evident. In 1953, for example, he collaborated with John Hope Franklin and C. Vann Woodward to provide research to bolster the NAACP landmark case *Brown v. Board of Education*. This research helped to undermine the legitimacy of the "separate but equal" doctrine of *Plessy v. Ferguson* and led to the beginning of racial desegregation of public schools throughout the United States.

But while the *Brown v. Board of Education* decision was embraced by broad segments of the population, it was rejected or ignored by many. And within just a few years, critics of desegregation resurrected the lingering eugenicist/hereditarian argument regarding the intellectual inferiority of African Americans.

"CAT ON A HOT TIN ROOF": BOND'S CHALLENGE TO A RESURGENCE OF EUGENICS

In 1958, Audrey Shuey published *The Testing of Negro Intelligence*. Shuey argued that her review of nearly three hundred studies of standardized intelligence tests had demonstrated "without a doubt" that black intelligence was inferior to that of white people.

Bond quickly responded to Shuey's work in a book review titled "Cat on a Hot Tin Roof" and leveled a scathing response. He reiterated many of the anti-eugenics arguments that he and others had made since the 1920s and then went on to note that Shuey's work was little more than a politically charged polemic.

BOND'S CRITIQUE OF RESURGENT RACISM

Bond wrote that her book was designed to fight school desegregation in Florida and was being made available to segregationist groups such as the White Citizen's Council of the United States free of charge! Later Shuey's dissertation advisor, Carleton Putnam, extended Shuey's eugenic approach with a redux of the old "mulatto argument," noting (incredibly) that because George Washington Carver had blue eyes, his great genius must have been due to his "white blood."

Bond challenged both Shuey and Putnam, noting that both had strong ties to white supremacist groups. These groups, he noted, would use any argument, however ridiculous, to demean the intelligence of African Americans and reject school desegregation.

RACIALLY STUFFED SHIRTS AND OTHER ENEMIES OF MANKIND

Bond continued to challenge the hereditarian/eugenicist interpretation of intelligence for the remainder of his life. In 1961, he wrote that Southern segregationists, who had once again resurrected the worn-out interpretations of the inherent intellectual inferiority of African Americans, were simply making another excuse against school desegregation.

In his parody of these segregationists' arguments titled "Racially Stuffed Shirts and Other Enemies of Mankind," Bond poked fun at both their lack of understanding of the broad literature on testing and the futility of the "Southern Manifesto"—an agreement to oppose any desegregation of society.

Using the same instrument employed by those pro-segregation politicians—the army Alpha tests—he noted that their voting constituency was in the lower 20 percent of mental ability, what they themselves had termed the "dull, normal, and moron category." Moreover, he pointed out that the signatories of the Southern Manifesto had attended colleges in the lowest 10 percent of all institutions of higher learning.

While Bond later regretted the viciousness of this attack, noting that it reflected his "indulgent foolishness," he effectively used this and other parodies to prove a point and challenge the specious eugenic interpretations of racist segregationist.

LATER LIFE OF HORACE MANN BOND

In the late 1960s, Horace Mann Bond continued his research on his final work: *Black American Scholars: A Study of their Beginnings*. He published this volume just before his death in 1972. The book was his final rejection of the hereditarian/eugenicist argument and a clear explication of his environmentalist position.

Bond demonstrated in his analysis of over one thousand black doctorates that many came from families of black professionals, what W. E. B. Du Bois had called the "talented tenth." But he also noted that a sizable group of black doctorates came from households of lower socioeconomic status, including poor farm families. While poor, these men and women had the benefit of involved parents who encouraged them to learn. They had excellent teachers and went to fine schools. These were the environmental qualities of success.

LEGACY

Horace Mann Bond shook the world of education on June 1, 1924, when, as a young man of nineteen years, he challenged the prevailing interpretations of differences in standardized intelligence test results. By rejecting the prevailing eugenicist/hereditarian interpretation of these results, he confronted the worn-out notions of white racial superiority, the inherent intellectual inferiority of African Americans and immigrants, as well as the pernicious ideas of eugenics.

Chapter Nine

Thurgood Marshall — The End of Legal Segregation

May 17, 1954

The long and difficult struggle of Africans Americans to achieve equality in America quietly began during slavery when both free blacks and slaves struggled to achieve identity and respect. Following the Civil War, three "Reconstruction Amendments" to the U.S. Constitution provided an early framework for this struggle by ending slavery (Thirteenth) providing basic civil rights (Fourteenth), and enfranchising African American men (Fifteenth).

FREEDMEN'S BUREAU SCHOOLS

But it was the Freedmen's Bureau Schools established in 1865 that offered newly freed black people in the South their first real opportunity for education. When Reconstruction ended in 1877 and white "Redeemers" in the South regained control, however, Freedmen's Bureau Schools closed and educational opportunities for African Americans virtually disappeared.

PLESSY V. FERGUSON

By the end of the century, the small gains in black education were once again dashed when the Supreme Court delivered its infamous "separate but equal" ruling of *Plessy v. Ferguson* in 1896.

**Figure 9.1. Thurgood Marshall, Associate Justice of the Supreme Court, 1976.
Source: Library of Congress's Prints and Photographs Division.**

Ironically, this major setback led to another important phase in the struggle for African American education with the establishment of the NAACP in 1909. This powerful civil rights group worked tirelessly within the legal system to challenge the *Plessy* decision and eventually helped to open the doors of schools throughout the nation to African Americans.

Then on May 17, 1954, Thurgood Marshall, chief consul for the NAACP, shook the world of education by successfully arguing before the U.S. Supreme Court that state-sponsored segregation of schools was unconstitutional. Marshall took the unprecedented position that racial segregation of public schools was a violation of the equal protection clause of the Fourteenth Amendment to the U.S. Constitution.

BROWN V. BOARD OF EDUCATION

The unanimous decision of the Warren Court in favor of racial desegregation that warm day in May was a major turning point for both the civil rights movement and the long struggle of educators to achieve racial justice in American public schools.

EARLY LIFE

Thurgood Marshall was born on July 2, 1908, in Baltimore, Maryland, during the most difficult period of Jim Crow. Thurgood was descended from slaves on both sides of his family. His father, William Canfield Marshall, was a railroad porter while his mother, Norma Arica Williams, was a teacher.

Thurgood grew up in what was essentially an upwardly mobile, middle-class household that promoted learning and respect for the U.S. Constitution. His father often took both Thurgood and his brothers to court to watch cases being debated and then after dinner would discuss them in lively debates.

INTRODUCTION TO THE LAW

Thurgood later would note that although his father never pressured him to become a lawyer, he "turned me into one . . . [by] teaching me to argue [and] by challenging my logic." Thurgood's career path was clear, not only as a skilled attorney but also as an advocate for individual and civil rights.

It was fitting that Thurgood attended Fredrick Douglass High School, named after the iconic civil rights figure who later he would idolize as a great hero. He graduated in 1925 in the top third of his class and then went on to Lincoln University in Pennsylvania. His application to the school noted that he intended to become as lawyer.

COLLEGE DAYS

But Thurgood was fun loving and a bit of a prankster during his college days. In fact, he was suspended from school twice for his misbehavior! Nevertheless, he joined the debate team and it was there that he slowly discovered his academic niche.

Though he was more interested in his social life and his membership in Alpha Phi Alpha social fraternity, Thurgood did join a protest against a local movie theater's segregation policy by participating in a sit-in.

MARRIAGE AND A NEW DIRECTION

During his senior year, however, his life changed dramatically when he married Vivien Buster Burey in September 1929. Perhaps because of Vivien's influence, Thurgood began to take his studies more seriously and he graduated from Lincoln with honors and a degree in American literature and philosophy.

Marshall's path to the law had now begun. Although he wanted to attend the University of Maryland School of Law, he did not even apply because of the school's strict segregation policy. Rather he was accepted to Howard Law where he was mentored by Charles Hamilton Houston, then dean of the school.

CHARLES HAMILTON HOUSTON: MENTOR

Dean Houston had a profound influence on young Thurgood. Houston was a veteran of World War I and was one of hundreds of young black soldiers (sometimes called "new Negros") who were decorated for bravery in the conflict.

Most of these young men assumed that their service to their country would help change racial policies back home. They were sadly mistaken. Typically when they returned home they were met with the same discrimination that they left behind before the war.

MODERN CIVIL RIGHTS MOVEMENT

The great disappointment of these men provided a core of protest that would eventually reignite the civil rights movement of the mid-twentieth century. Houston once said that because of his experiences in Europe, if he ever returned alive, he would dedicate his life to eliminating racial discrimination.

Dean Houston saw something in young Thurgood Marshall. He recognized what appeared to be a burning desire to change the world and together he and Thurgood would do just that.

THURGOOD JOINS THE NAACP: *MURRAY V. PEARSON*

Under the watchful eye of Houston, Thurgood Marshall graduated from Howard Law in 1933, first in his class. With the urging of Houston, Thurgood joined the NAACP and in 1934 became part of Houston's legal team challenging segregation policies that had blocked African Americans from attending law school. The pivotal case in this struggle was *Murray v. Pearson*.

Thurgood represented Donald Gaines Murray, an African American Amherst College graduate who had been denied admission to the University of Maryland School of Law because of its segregation policy. Certainly this case must have struck a chord with Thurgood given that he too had faced these policies just a few years before.

PLESSY V. FERGUSON AS AN ARGUMENT

Marshall employed a legal strategy developed by Nathan Margold, the prominent civil rights attorney and author of the influential "Margold Report." Margold argued that by denying African Americans the right to attend the all-white University of Maryland School of Law, they had violated the infamous *Plessy v. Ferguson* decision.

The Maryland Court of Appeals ruled in favor of Murray and against the state, noting that Maryland had not provided African Americans "equal" facilities. The court wrote, "Compliance with the constitution cannot be deferred at the will of the state."

Marshall had won his first major victory and thus helped to open the doors of law schools to black people not only in Maryland but eventually throughout the nation. Black attorneys that graduated from Maryland and other law schools during this period would provide the core of opposition to racial segregation and discrimination for the next half century.

LEGAL DEFENSE AND EDUCATIONAL FUND

Fresh from his victory in the case *Murray v. Pearson*, Marshall worked with lawyers in the NAACP to develop a strategy to fight racial injustice within the framework of the legal system. Then in 1940, along with Houston and others, he founded the NAACP Legal Defense and Educational Fund, today known as the LDF.

Because of his judicial success and his leadership in the organization of the LDF, Marshall became its first executive director. As such he recruited a cadre of young black lawyers into the organization and began to systematically challenge the foundation of the Jim Crow laws.

MARSHALL AND THE SUPREME COURT

Over the next decade Marshall successfully argued numerous landmark civil rights cases before the U.S. Supreme Court that challenged Jim Crow. These included *Smith v. Allwright* in 1944, *Shelley v. Kraemer* in 1948, and *McLaurin v. Oklahoma* in 1950.

Smith v. Allwright was an early voting rights case that challenged a Texas law prohibiting African Americans from voting in primary elections. In *Shelley v. Kraemer* the court overturned racial covenants that discriminated against African Americans, and then in *McLaurin v. Oklahoma* Marshall argued successfully against policies at Oklahoma State University that segregated white and black graduate students.

The heady experience of standing before the justices of the Supreme Court and arguing successfully for racial justice was an inspiration to others who would follow his lead. It also prepared Marshall for perhaps his biggest challenge and most successful struggle: *Brown v. Board of Education of Topeka Kansas*.

BROWN V. BOARD OF EDUCATION—BACKGROUND

The case of *Brown v. Board of Education* was a relatively simple one on the surface but would strike a nerve with the American people and launch the modern civil rights movement.

The story began in 1951 when six-year-old Linda Brown asked her father, the Reverend Oliver Brown, a simple question. Why did she have to attend the Public School for Negroes that required a long walk and then a bus ride when there was an all-white school close to her home?

It was difficult to explain the complex situation of racial injustice to Linda, but nevertheless he attempted to enroll her at the white school. Linda was turned away because she was black.

EARLY SETBACKS FOR BROWN

One can only imagine the disappointment of the Brown family and the local black community in general. Reverend Brown sought support from like-minded African American progressives and with twelve other parents sued the Topeka Board of Education.

As expected, the court ruled in favor of the board and against Brown using the "separate but equal doctrine" as the basis of their verdict. A special three-judge panel ruled that because "white and negro schools were substantially equal," Linda Brown was not being discriminated against and therefore could not attend the white school.

MARSHALL AND THE LDF JOIN THE STRUGGLE

It was at this point that the NAACP LDF lawyers, headed by Marshall, appealed the decision to the U.S. Supreme Court. In December 1952, Marshall argued that not allowing African American children to attend all-white schools was a violation of the equal protection clause embedded in the Fourteenth Amendment to the U.S. Constitution.

A NEW STRATEGY—THE FOURTEENTH AMENDMENT

This strategy was new and ultimately successful. In other cases, such as the *Murray* decision, two decades before, Marshall had used *Plessy v. Ferguson* to convince the court to desegregate the University of Maryland School of Law. This strategy was now being abandoned in favor of a new approach using the equal protection clause of the Fourteenth Amendment as the basis of the argument. It was a gamble.

The Fourteenth Amendment to the U.S. Constitution was passed in the heat of early Reconstruction following the Civil War. It clearly stated that "no state shall deny . . . to any person within its jurisdiction the equal protection of the laws." Moreover, Section 5 of the amendment gave Congress the power to enforce this provision "with appropriate legislation."

THE U.S. CONSTITUTION: LIVING DOCUMENT OR ORIGINAL INTENT?

The problem was the apparent vagueness of the Fourteenth Amendment. Those, like Marshall, who perceived the Constitution as a "living document" that must be reinterpreted over the years in light of social, political, and economic change argued that school segregation laws were a clear violation of civil rights.

Those who read the Constitution as a more static document based on the "original intent" of the framers (like the pro-segregation attorneys) claimed that because the Fourteenth Amendment did not mention the issue of school segregation, it was clearly a state matter.

FIRST ARGUMENT REGARDING *BROWN V. BOARD OF EDUCATION*

The segregation cases were first presented before the Court in December 1952, and the nine justices listened to each of the arguments but deferred any decision. The case would be scheduled for reargument during the next term, beginning in October 1953.

FIVE QUESTIONS

In the meantime, each side was instructed to address five questions. The first three of these involved the "original intent" of the Fourteenth Amendment. While the amendment did not mention school segregation per se, other cases had used the Fourteenth Amendment to strike down discriminatory state laws regarding the composition of juries and transportation issues.

Marshall felt that because the Fourteenth Amendment had been used in these cases, school segregation laws clearly could be understood as part of the intent of the amendment, even if not stated explicitly.

The third and fourth questions presented to the attorneys on both sides had to do with "how and when" desegregation would proceed. Marshall wanted immediate action from the Court but admitted that logistical difficulties as well as the cultural and political rejection of desegregation in the South might slow that process.

THE 1954 *BROWN* DECISION—IMPORTANT BUT VAGUE

After much deliberation, the nine justices unanimously ruled that state school segregation laws, based on the *Plessy v. Ferguson* decision of 1896, were unconstitutional. These laws were a violation of the Fourteenth Amendment even if black and white schools were deemed "equal." The questions of "how and when" desegregation would take place, however, were absent from the ruling.

The justices understood that the issue of school desegregation was a volatile one. Numerous communities throughout the South immediately began to challenge the ruling through legal means, violent protest, and simple political "foot dragging."

THE NEED FOR COMPROMISE

As a result, the justices felt that a compromise was necessary. The compromise they developed would allow individual states to determine how to proceed with the desegregation process, but lower courts would determine whether they were acting in good faith to implement this monumental ruling.

After much deliberation and apparent "arm twisting" by Chief Justice Warren, on May 31, 1955, just a little over a year since the May 17, 1954, decision, the Court ruled on the question of how and when desegregation of schools would take place.

THE 1955 DECISION: "WITH ALL DELIBERATE SPEED"

The Court ruled that individual state cases were "remanded to the District Courts to take such proceedings and enter such orders and decrees consistent with this opinion (the May 17 ruling) . . . with all deliberate speed."

The NAACP's decades-long effort to end racial segregation of schools had been successful. Marshall and his cadre of lawyers had achieved a major victory in their efforts to challenge a fundamental component of Jim Crow.

Racial segregation, however, would "not go quietly into the night." In the years following the two monumental *Brown* decisions regarding the desegregation of schools, Marshall and the LDF had their work cut out for them.

MAJOR PROBLEMS: DE JURE AND DE FACTO SEGREGATION

Marshall and the LDF faced two major problems. The first was the virulent political opposition to desegregation manifested in a variety of legal and sometimes extralegal tactics to slow or block the integration of schools. Laws that blocked desegregation orders, often referred to as *de jure* segregation, were common during this period.

The second problem was the fact that many communities throughout the United States were residentially segregated. As a result, schools in these areas were racially segregated as well. This form of segregation was referred to as *de facto* segregation because it was due to the residential patterns of communities.

LITTLE ROCK NINE AND GOVERNOR FAUBUS

In 1958, the LDF under the leadership of Marshall challenged Arkansas governor Orval Faubus's tactics that interfered with the desegregation of Little Rock Central High School.

A year earlier, nine black students had attempted to enroll in the high school, but the governor dispatched the Arkansas National Guard to prevent them from entering. In response, President Eisenhower sent troops from the 101st Airborne Division of the U.S. Army to escort the nine students into the school. In addition, he federalized the Arkansas National Guard so that the governor no longer had control over them.

DIFFICULTIES FOR THE LITTLE ROCK NINE

The Little Rock Nine, as they were called, were allowed to attend Central High but they experienced violence, humiliation, and physical abuse. Melba

Pattillo, for example, had acid thrown in her eyes and later she was trapped in a bathroom stall while white girls dropped flaming pieces of paper on her.

In another incident, Minnijean Brown was verbally taunted by a group of white boys in the school lunchroom. The abuse was so vicious that Minnijean walked over to the boys and poured her chili on them. She was suspended for six days while the boys were not reprimanded.

COOPER V. AARON — STATES MUST COMPLY

When the school year finally ended, Orval Faubus once again acted to prevent further integration of the school by petitioning the Supreme Court to delay the desegregation of the schools for two and one-half years.

In the resulting case, *Cooper v. Aaron*, Marshall and the LDF argued against the petition and the court agreed. The ruling was that states must adhere to Supreme Court decisions (in this case *Brown v. Board of Education*) even if they disagreed with them.

Faubus responded by calling a special session of the state legislature to challenge the ruling, and as a result all four public high schools in Little Rock were closed. The governor successfully appealed to the people of Little Rock to pass a special referendum that would lease the four high schools to private institutions in order to maintain segregation. This plan was rejected in turn by the court, leading to months of violence and disorder. This was called the "lost year" of public schooling in Little Rock.

THE LDF IN THE 1960S

The LDF would continue its important work during the 1960s, though Marshall was tapped by President Kennedy for the U.S. Court of Appeals and later by President Johnson to serve as a Supreme Court justice. In 1961, the LDF successfully argued for the desegregation of the University of Georgia in *Holmes v. Danner* in the U.S. District Court for the Middle District of Georgia.

Then in 1962, they fought for the admission of James Meredith at the University of Mississippi. The *Meredith v. Fair* decision of the U.S. District Court for the Southern District of Mississippi struck down an existing Jim Crow segregation law (de jure segregation), and Meredith entered the University of Mississippi. He completed his degree the following year and became an outspoken civil rights activist.

DE FACTO SEGREGATION AND BUSSING

While the LDF had success challenging *de jure* segregation, *de facto* segregation was another matter. Here the remedy appeared to be student bussing. But the idea of bussing black students to white schools and white students to black schools was rejected by many communities as well as political leaders throughout the south.

In 1956, for example, Southern "dixiecrats" led by South Carolina senator Strom Thurmond formed a coalition of over one hundred congressmen and senators to issue what is often referred to as the Southern Manifesto. This manifesto, formally known as "The Declaration of Constitutional Principles," was designed to oppose desegregation of schools by all available means. This of course included opposition to the bussing of students.

SCHOOL CLOSURES AND "FREEDOM OF CHOICE"

Virginia's senator, Harry Byrd, for example, called for "massive resistance" to the *Brown* decision and bussing. Virginia in turn passed a series of laws to prevent desegregation. This action led to the closing of many schools.

In 1959, Prince Edward County, Virginia, refused desegregation orders and closed all its public schools until 1964 when the Court forced their compliance. During this period, however, white students often received tuition grants to attend private schools sometimes referred to as "segregation academies." Black students, on the other hand, were often left with no access to education at all.

THE "FREEDOM OF CHOICE" TACTIC

Another tactic was the "Freedom of Choice" strategy used throughout the South. Here communities such as New Kent County in eastern Virginia (the greater Richmond area) developed a plan that allowed both black and white students to "choose" the high school they wished to attend.

The result was that only two black students chose to attend a white school while no white students chose to attend a black school. As a result, the racial composition of these schools, as well as others throughout the South, remained largely unchanged throughout the late 1950s and early 1960s.

THE LDF AND TWO LANDMARK DECISIONS

Following the passage of the landmark Civil Rights Law in 1964 and then the Voting Rights Act the following year, the Supreme Court made two important rulings that directly affected the issue of bussing.

The first was the LDF-sponsored 1968 case of *Green v. County School Board of New Kent County* that rejected their "Freedom of Choice" plan. The Court unambiguously ordered the county (and others that had adopted similar plans) to desegregate immediately to eliminate racial discrimination "root and branch."

The second case that directly involved the bussing issue was the 1971 *Swan v. Charlotte-Mecklenburg Board of Education*. This decision upheld "intradistrict" bussing to achieve desegregation of public schools. Although this decision would be challenged for the next three decades, it effectively signaled the beginning of the end of *de facto* segregation within school districts and allowed bussing to achieve racial balance.

LOOPHOLE: INTERDISTRICT SEGREGATION

Nevertheless, segregation of schools in both the North and South remained a problem because there had been no court ruling that outlawed interdistrict segregation. In other words, segregation of schools still existed across district lines.

In Detroit, Michigan, for example, the lower federal court sought to eliminate this problem by allowing bussing between the generally black inner city to the predominately white suburbs.

This ruling was challenged and the Supreme Court ruled in *Milliken v. Bradley* (1974) that federal courts did not have the authority to order interdistrict bussing to achieve racial desegregation unless it was demonstrated that suburban school districts had intentionally mandated segregation through law. It should be noted that Thurgood Marshall was one of the minority Supreme Court justices dissenting on this ruling.

WHITE FLIGHT AND "UNITARY STATUS"

The result of the *Milliken* decision was an upsurge in "white flight" in which white families often left inner cities and moved to the suburbs to avoid sending their children to integrated schools. This phenomenon continues to the present day.

Moreover, by the 1990s a more conservative Supreme Court began to relax its rules regarding bussing to achieve racial balance in schools. In a number of decisions, the Court allowed school districts to be relieved from Court supervision "once they had eliminated segregation" and achieved what was called "unitary status."

Using the policy of unitary status, the Supreme Court ruled in *Belk v. Charlotte Mecklenburg Board of Education* (2002) that because the school system had achieved "desegregation status," bussing was no longer necessary. This decision effectively overturned the *Swann* decision of 1971.

As a result of the new, conservative posture of the Court, white flight to the suburbs, as well as the emergence of charter schools, magnet schools, and home schooling, the progress toward racial desegregation has slowed.

SCHOOL CONSOLIDATION AND INCREASED RACIAL CONTACT

Recent research, however, has demonstrated that policies of school consolidation in states such as North Carolina may result in greater racial contact between black people and white people.

In the past decade, North Carolina has reduced the number of school districts from 175 to 115. This consolidation has increased "racial integration" in these schools. In short there appears to be some prospect of increased interactions between white students and black students in public schools in this troubled time of political polarization.

MARSHALL: FEDERAL JURIST AND ASSOCIATE JUSTICE OF THE SUPREME COURT

While the LDF continued its work in the area of desegregation and civil rights, its founder and leader Thurgood Marshall would begin his distinguished career as a federal jurist and eventually an associate justice on the Supreme Court.

Impressed with his important work in the area of desegregation and civil rights over the years, especially his founding of the LDF and his active role in the landmark *Brown v. Board of Education*, President John F. Kennedy appointed Thurgood Marshall to the U.S. Court of Appeals for the Second Circuit.

Though a group of senators led by James Eastland from Mississippi temporarily blocked his nomination, he was eventually confirmed and served on that body until 1965.

SOLICITOR GENERAL AND JUSTICE OF THE SUPREME COURT

Then in 1965, President Lyndon B. Johnson appointed Marshall as the U.S. Solicitor General, where the civil rights leader argued many cases successfully for the federal government before the Supreme Court.

His success in this position led to his nomination to the Supreme Court in June 1967 where he was confirmed two months later by a Senate vote of sixty-nine to eleven. Thurgood Marshall was the first African American to hold this position, and he served successfully on the court for the next quarter-century until his retirement in 1991.

LEGACY

Thurgood Marshall was a beacon of hope for a more racially equitable world. As an activist with the NAACP, founder and leader of the LDF, and a progressive associate justice of the Supreme Court, he helped to bring the issue of racial inequality to the attention of the American people.

But Thurgood Marshall will always be remembered as the man who shook the world of education by successfully arguing the landmark case of *Brown v. Board of Education* before the Supreme Court in 1954 and 1955. The world will never be the same as a result.

Chapter Ten

The Kids are All Right—Political Activism

February 14, 2018

By the turn of the twenty-first century, American public education had become a well-established component of modern society. Over the years, American educators had developed innovative curricular approaches and had addressed many of the goals of early reformers. Now education was open to all, irrespective of gender, race, ethnicity, or religious background.

DEADLY PROBLEM FOR PUBLIC SCHOOLS

Of course, the system was far from perfect and education continued to face some fundamental problems. Then, almost inexplicably, it was plagued with another challenge—and this time it was deadly: mass shootings of students.

The massacre of students at Columbine High School in 1999 was an ominous sign of things to come. But after two decades of inaction on the part of local, state, and federal officials and persistent hand wringing by cultural, political, and economic leaders, the carnage has continued.

A NEW SAINT VALENTINE'S DAY MASSACRE

Then on Valentine's Day, February 14, 2018, the kids of Marjory Stoneman Douglas High School in Parkland, Florida, shook the world of education when they defiantly challenged the status quo on gun violence and declared "enough is enough."

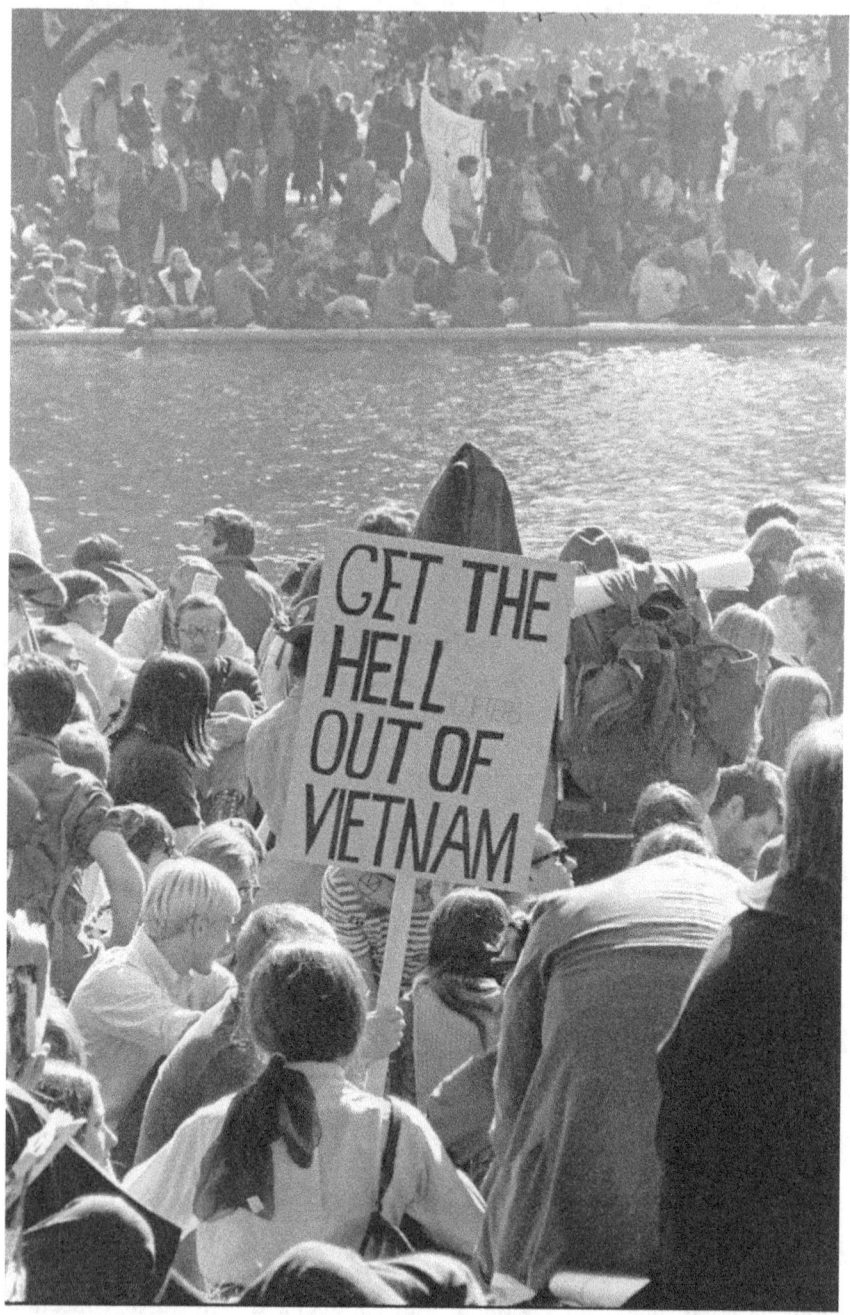

Figure 10.1. Student Protesters against the War in Vietnam, 1968. Source: University of Wisconsin Digital Collections.

On that fateful day, a former student of Marjory Stoneman Douglas High School walked into the suburban school, opened fire with his AR-15 semi-automatic weapon, and within minutes murdered seventeen students.

What followed was a scene that we have unfortunately become accustomed to in the past two decades: hundreds of young kids running for their lives, screaming and crying with their hands raised high in the air.

ENOUGH IS ENOUGH

But a handful of students remained defiant and angry. They were outraged at what they saw as the typical response to this horrific act of violence: the interviews of weeping children, mothers, and fathers; the media frenzy capturing the chaos of the moment; and the nearly ritualistic expressions of "thoughts and prayers" coming from local, state, and national officials.

THE PARKLAND KIDS

Among those angry and defiant students were David Hogg, Emma Gonzalez, and Cameron Kasky. Each had lost friends and fellow students, and each stood before the media that morning demanding an immediate change to our federal gun safety laws.

For these kids, the National Rifle Association (NRA) lobby had paralyzed our political system to the point that even the most sensible gun safety legislation was either ignored or ridiculed. Indeed, enough was enough.

Within hours, the message of #neveragain reverberated through social media, rallying thousands of kids throughout the country to take a stand on gun safety. The stage was set for a grassroots challenge to the inaction of our political leaders.

MARCH FOR OUR LIVES ROAD TOUR

By the summer of 2018, the movement had gained enormous strength and led to the remarkable "March for Our Lives: Road Tour." The inspirational tour eventually reached sixty-eight cities across the nation. The example of these fearless students empowered thousands of others to demand change from their political representatives and "do something."

David Hogg summarized the frustration and anger that many of his fellow students felt as they prepared to go to school each day. He said, "For too long we have looked to elected officials to solve America's gun violence crisis and time and time again, they have fallen to the pressure of NRA donations and the status quo. Their failure to do their jobs has had deadly consequences."

As part of their grassroots movement, the kids of Parkland and others developed what they called a Peace Plan for a Safer America. This proposal went beyond the futile calls to political leaders and created a blueprint to understand the causes of gun violence and develop a real dialogue among Americans of all ages regarding this growing epidemic.

THE "PEACE PLAN"

Among the recommendations of the Peace Plan were a national registry system for firearms, an all-out ban on military grade assault weapons, a ban on high-capacity magazines, a system of "red flag laws" to disarm individuals who pose a threat to their community and to themselves, and a national firearms "buy-back" program.

The Peace Plan also recommended that the Federal Election Commission and the IRS investigate the NRA for illegal lobbying activity and the misuse of their tax-free status.

KIDS DEMANDING CHANGE – A HISTORY

While the ultimate result of the Peace Plan and the grassroots campaign of young Americans is not yet known, it has garnered support from some congressional representatives, presidential candidates, and thousands of Americans across the country.

What is clear, however, is that the kids from Parkland shook the world of education on that sunny but tragic Valentine's Day in 2018 and demonstrated to the nation that individual and collective action—even by a small group of students—can initiate social and political change.

A LONG HISTORY OF KIDS MAKING A DIFFERENCE

While we celebrate the fearlessness of the Parkland kids, it is important to remember that throughout the history of American education, kids themselves have often demanded and succeeded in making a difference.

Beginning in the nineteenth century when students often challenged and then helped to change the severe disciplinary policies of schoolmasters through the early twentieth century when kids fought against the arbitrary policies of administrators to the mid-twentieth century when they demanded fundamental changes in students' legal status, the kids have been all right!

STUDENTS CHALLENGE CORPORAL PUNISHMENT

From the beginning of our nation's history, severe discipline was the centerpiece of classroom management. Rooted in the Judeo-Christian idea of original sin, children were seen as stained, perhaps even evil. As a result, severe corporal punishment was typically perceived as the appropriate way to manage children.

The biblical imperative of "spare the rod and spoil the child" first appeared in Proverbs 23: 13–14 and noted clearly that one should "withhold not correction from the child . . . for if thou beatest him with a rod . . . thou shall deliver his soul from hell."

A CHALLENGE TO CORPORAL PUNISHMENT

By the eighteenth century, there was a growing sense that corporal punishment was the worst sort of discipline, but whipping children continued to be common practice at home and in schools. As we have seen, while these attitudes were challenged by such figures as John Locke, Jean-Jacques Rousseau, Joseph Lancaster, Emma Willard, and many others, a vicious culture of violence persisted.

While it is important to recognize the intellectual giants who promoted more humane forms of discipline over the years, we should also remember that it was often the students themselves who challenged the system and eventually helped to make change.

A WHIPPING IN THE 1820s

John Dean Caton, future justice of the Illinois Supreme Court, admitted in his memoir that although he seldom used corporal punishment while a teacher in the 1820s, he did experience a near rebellion from a group of students who "challenged his authority" and his use of the rod. Caton "resolved to settle the question of who was master."

On his way to school the next day, he cut a few birch switches "about five feet long and as large as my thumb at the butt." When he arrived at the school, he demanded that the leader of the rebellion "stand forth" for punishment. He applied ten blows to the child as hard as he could then struck him over the head and in the face.

But the "leader" was not remorseful enough and so Caton continued the beating. He took out a fresh whip and laid fifteen lashes "with his best effort [until] the cotton from the student's shirt flew across the house in bits."

Chapter 10

STUDENT PASSIVE AGGRESSION

While the "delinquent" had been temporarily subdued, the boys in the class were determined to challenge the schoolmaster. For the rest of the short semester they mocked Caton and used collective passive aggression toward him until he finally left the school.

STUDENTS REBEL

Another nineteenth-century schoolteacher, John Vance Cheyney, often used corporal punishment on his students in West Rupert, New York. Cheyney wrote in his autobiography that his use of violence in the school eventually led to an uprising. He noted that his students had "turned against him."

Cheyney resolved to maintain order and "chucked the shortest of them . . . with my feet on his neck." But this action merely strengthened the resolve of other boys in the class. Sensing further "rebellion," Cheyney punished one "strapping dullard" who continued to look out the window. He "struck him across the jugular vein with the back of a solid book." By the end of the week Cheyney had only one student left in the class, and he was not rehired.

MR. AUGUSTUS STAR—STUDENTS ARE FED UP

And then we have the story of Mr. Augustus Star. Warren Burton, the nineteenth-century pedagogue, wrote that in his "tenth winter in school" Mr. Star was hired as the new schoolmaster. Although he was "dressed genteelly and [was] gentlemanly in his manners," the former privateer officer during the War of 1812 used extreme violence on his charges.

On one occasion, Burton wrote that Star knocked one lad down and hurled a stick of wood at another. When his students challenged him, he simply became more violent. Star's reputation in the community grew, and soon "some parents kept their younger children at home."

MR. STAR GOES TOO FAR

One day, Burton wrote that Mr. Star struck John Howe on the head with a ruler, giving the boy "a cut . . . which drew blood." The screaming boy and the dripping blood were a call to action. John's older brother Thomas and his friend Mark Mouton attacked Mr. Star, wrestled the ruler from his hand, and with the help of several other boys carried him out of the schoolhouse, "kicking and swearing."

The entire classroom followed, each in their own way protesting the violent teacher. The boys carried Mr. Star to the crest of a hill, "smooth and slippery as pure ice from a recent rain . . . and pitched him over the side."

DOWN THE ICY HILL

Star slid down the hill "until he fairly came to the climax . . . of his pedagogical career." The captain looked up to see what Burton called the "mutinous crew, great and small male and female, now lining the side of the road" next to the hill. Star gradually picked himself up, returned to the schoolhouse, gathered up his belongings, and the next day he "sailed out of port never to be seen again."

Certainly not all nineteenth-century students resorted to what Burton called "mutiny" to challenge the whipping, torture, and violence of some schoolmasters. But the literature is full of examples of this kind of behavior. Students would endure a great deal. But once a teacher crossed the line, they often challenged him passively or aggressively.

Their collective actions over the years, combined with new ideas of humane discipline promoted by a handful of philosophers and educators, gradually put an end to the whipping post and limited the use of the ferule and the paddle. And while corporal punishment is still sanctioned in some communities today, routine violence against children at home and in the classroom has begun to disappear.

STUDENTS CHALLENGE SCHOOL ADMINISTRATIVE POLICY

Challenging corporal punishment of schoolteachers was common in the nineteenth century, but students also demanded changes in some school administration policies.

A good example of this sort of spontaneous protest can be seen in early twentieth-century Chicago. During this critical period of curricular and administrative change, Chicago public schools developed a new organizational scheme often referred to as the "Harper Plan," named after William Rainey Harper, then president of the University of Chicago.

OPPOSITION TO THE HARPER PLAN

The Harper Plan was similar to other school reorganization/consolidation plans that had swept across the nation during this period. School boards were often restructured, and typically local members were replaced by businessmen from the community.

Similarly, principals were hired from outside the school and their selection was based solely on educational attainment rather than the traditional method of promoting an experienced teacher to principal from within the school.

These changes were often challenged by local schoolteachers and students, as well as the imposition of new educational "standards" in the classroom that sometimes resulted in student strikes and walkouts.

THE CLARKE SCHOOL "REBELLION" OF 1902

During the academic year 1902–1903, a new teacher from the Clarke school on Chicago's near north side announced to her class that all math tests must be "perfect" or they would fail. After some grumbling, a spontaneous chant of "no one is perfect" erupted from the class.

The large class then walked out of the school and continued their chant. The newly appointed principal backed up the teacher, though he eventually allowed the students to return to their classroom. The students then staged a "victory parade" and were joined by members of the community.

DEFEAT TURNED TO VICTORY

Their victory, however, was short lived. When the newly installed Superintendant Cooley heard of the "rebellion," he sent what the *Chicago Tribune* called a "squad of truant officers" to the school. By day's end, over two hundred students had been detained. Dozens of mothers then stormed the school and reportedly "threw mud" at the truant officers.

While the Clarke School Rebellion soon ended with a compromise on both sides, it was clear that students had been heard. They had helped to change educational policy in a small but meaningful way.

THE ANDREW JACKSON SCHOOL INCIDENT

The same academic year as the Clarke School Rebellion, Janie McKeon, an experienced teacher from Andrew Jackson School, was suspended by a newly installed principal. McKeon had disciplined a student from her class of fifty-five students because he had used abusive language. Inexplicably the principal reinstated the student. But McKeon refused to admit him, and she was then suspended for thirty-five days for her insubordination.

A STUDENT STRIKE

The incident was far from over. Students from the school who supported the popular teacher went on strike. Hundreds marched to the home of their alderman, the infamous Johnny Powers, who sided with the students and forced Superintendent Cooley to reinstate the teacher.

Once again, the spontaneous actions of students had made a difference, however small. Though they had few rights in the classroom, they forced change through their actions, deeds, chants, walkouts, and strikes.

CHALLENGES TO *IN LOCO PARENTIS*: THE 1960s AND 1970s

And yet it was their lack of basic rights that mobilized students during the mid-twentieth century and challenged longstanding policies of *in loco parentis*. What this meant of course was that students had few if any constitutional rights but rather the schools and school districts determined those "rights" as if they were their parents.

During the late 1960s and 1970s, however, things began to change for students. In the wake of the civil rights movement, the antiwar movement, the women's liberation movement, and the individual rights movements of this period, many students felt empowered to challenge school policies and demanded their basic rights under the U.S. Constitution.

TINKER V. DES MOINES: FREE SPEECH

One of the earliest challenges to this longstanding principle of *in loco parentis* came in December 1965. Several students from Des Moines, Iowa, including John and Mary Beth Tinker and Christopher Eckert, wore black armbands to protest the War in Vietnam. The principals of their two schools were angered by this demonstration and suspended the trio for a violation of unspecified school rules.

The three students then sued their school boards, arguing that they had been deprived of their First Amendment right of free speech. The suit was initially dismissed by a district court but in appeal it went all the way to the U.S. Supreme Court.

The ultimate decision, *Tinker v. Des Moines*, upheld the students' right of free speech to protest the war. Associate Justice Fortas wrote, "the armbands did not cause a disturbance [and] teachers and students do not shed their constitutional rights at the schoolhouse gate."

GOSS V. LOPEZ: DUE PROCESS RIGHTS

Another important turning point in this struggle was led by Dwight Lopez and nine other students at Central High School in Columbus, Ohio. In this case, the students were not protesting the war or demanding changes in civil rights laws but rather challenged the school board's decision to suspend Lopez without a hearing because of an altercation he had in the school lunchroom.

Dwight Lopez, with the support of the other nine students, argued that he had been deprived of his right of due process under the Fourteenth Amendment to the Constitution. The case eventually came before the Supreme Court. The court ruled that schools do not have the right to deprive students of their education without due process. *Goss v. Lopez* reinforced the earlier *Tinker* decision and significantly promoted the individual rights of students.

WOOD V. STRICKLAND: STUDENTS' RIGHT TO SUE MEMBERS OF THE SCHOOL BOARD

That same year, there was another important moment in the struggle to challenge *in loco parentis*: the *Wood v. Strickland* decision. In this case two tenth-grade girls (Peggy and Virginia) from Mena Public High School in Arkansas "spiked" the punch (with two bottles of malt liquor) at a home economics function.

Peggy and Virginia were suspended for the remainder of the semester (about three months). But neither the girls nor their parents were allowed to attend the suspension hearing. With help from their parents, the girls challenged this action in court and argued that their civil rights and due process under the law had been violated.

The case was finally settled by the Supreme Court in the *Wood v. Strickland* decision and was followed up by a federal court ruling that gave students the right to sue individual members of the school board but not the board as a whole.

Although the "spiked punch" case, as it is often referred to, did not transform students' rights, it did help to open the door just enough to encourage other students to challenge the basis of *in loco parentis*.

BELLINGER V. LUND: STRIP SEARCHES ARE UNCONSTITUTIONAL

About that same time, two elementary school students, Cassandra and Onieka, were accused of stealing $4.50 from another student. They were brought to the restroom and, according to the students, were ordered to take off their clothes including their socks and shoes. They also claimed that they were ordered to "pull down their underpants," though the teacher disputed that claim.

The girls, with the help of their parents, sued the school district for unlawful search and seizure, claiming that they had been "strip searched." The Supreme Court ruled in *Bellinger v. Lund* (1977) that these sorts of searches are permissible in schools only "where there is a threat of imminent serious harm."

IMMINENT SERIOUS HARM—SEARCHES FOR GUNS AND DRUGS

While this clearly was a victory for Cassandra and Onieka, school boards have used the language of this decision to allow them to search lockers for drugs and guns. In these cases, a school can reasonably argue that a search was necessary because there was a threat of imminent harm.

DRUG TESTING—IMMINENT SERIOUS HARM?

And yet the issue of drug testing is another matter. In the more conservative 1980s, a number of school districts, including one in Veronia, Oregon, established a policy of drug testing all student athletes. In this case, seventh-grader James Acton challenged this ruling in the courts.

But despite opposition from members of the school sport teams and the student body in general, the Supreme Court ruled in *Veronia v. Acton* that testing student athletes for drugs was constitutional because schools were "guardians and tutors of children entrusted to their care."

This ruling, reminiscent of the idea of *in loco parentis*, established a major precedent regarding the role of schools as "guardians of children." Nevertheless, students have made significant progress in individual rights since the 1960s.

STUDENT RIGHTS TODAY

Today students have the right to free public education and parents do not have to pay real estate taxes or be citizens in order for their children to receive that education (*Plyler v. Doe*). In addition, homeless students, students with disabilities, and girls who are pregnant also have the right to attend school.

These basic rights, of course, are guaranteed by constitutional provisions such as the "equal protection clause" and implied by the First and Fourteenth Amendments to the U.S. Constitution. Other rights are embedded in state constitutions and Supreme Court decisions. Still others such as the Individuals with Disabilities Education Act, the McKinney-Vento Homeless Assistance Act, and Title IX of the Civil Rights Act are federally mandated to assure that all students have access to education.

THE LEGACY OF STUDENT PROTEST

But while these basic rights to educational opportunities were promoted by the Founding Fathers and progressive statesmen at both the state and federal level, it is also clear that students themselves have fought, in their own way, to secure them.

The ongoing struggle, beginning in the early nineteenth century, that challenged vicious corporal punishment is a good example. While still legal today in nearly two dozen states, the whipping post and the capricious use of the switch and the ferule have gradually disappeared from most of the classrooms of America in part because of the brave actions of young students.

Challenges to curricular and administrative policies during the early school consolidation period were common. Students often defied capricious curricular changes or the firing of a beloved teacher or principal with walkouts, strikes, or perpetual passive aggression.

By the mid-twentieth century, students began to protest the age-old school culture of *in loco parentis* through the courts. These actions led to the right to due process and the right to sue individuals on school boards.

As a result of their actions during this period, students achieved limited rights of free speech. Political speech has generally been protected, though understandably it cannot be aggressive or disrupt the school. Students also cannot make sexual remarks or suggestive innuendos.

In short, while the actions of these and many other students throughout our educational history have promoted important changes in disciplinary policies in classrooms and have made major inroads into the age-old culture of *in loco parentis*, there is much left to do.

PARKLAND KIDS: FROM THE COURTS TO THE STREETS

The actions of the Parkland kids, however, have taken students out of the classroom and into the streets once again. They argue that gun violence, especially in American schools, is a disgrace, and the inability of either the courts or political leaders to deal with this issue has moved these young men and women in a new direction.

AN OLD SICKNESS BECOMES A PLAGUE

School violence has, of course, been a feature of American schools since the nineteenth century, but these early episodes were often due to arguments that went wrong; parent, teacher, or principal disputes over whipping their children; and later because of gang violence.

With the horrific tower shooting at the University of Texas at Austin in 1964, however, the nature of violence seemed to change. And with the Columbine High School Massacre we clearly witnessed the beginning a sustained period of mass killings that had previously been unknown.

ELEVEN MASS SHOOTINGS

Since that terrible day in the spring of 1999, there have been hundreds of school shootings across the United States. Of those, eleven have been classified as mass shootings by the FBI. These include the deadliest school shooting in American history at Virginia Tech University in April 2007 when thirty-one students were killed and the grisly Sandy Hook massacre of twenty-six elementary school students and their teachers as they lay huddled on the floor screaming and crying.

Others on this awful list include the Parkland Valentine's Day massacre of seventeen and the Santa Fe High shooting of 2018 that killed ten and many others. It's important to remember, once again, that these gruesome mass shooting have happened in the past decades since 1999.

"NEVER AGAIN"

In this context, the words of David Hogg "never again" clearly resonate. Hogg like other Parkland kids and kids throughout America for that matter live in a world much different from the one many of us remember.

While some of us may recall with a certain amount of humor the famous "duck and cover" exercises of the 1950s and 1960s, we never experienced the terror of mass shootings. And while some parents of the Cold War era built their own private bomb shelters, the reality is that we never had to use them.

The kids of America have been exposed to danger that is nearly inconceivable. The daily listing of horrific gun violence and the inaction of political and civic leaders has left them with no alternative but to "take it to the streets."

Like generations of students before them, they have "had enough" and have banded together to force educational change. Learning the lessons from the kids who challenged corporal punishment, capricious educational policies, the fundamental injustice of *in loco parentis*, as well as the success of civil rights and the anti-Vietnam War movements, these kids have taken a stand for educational change. And yes, the kids are all right!

Conclusion

Although it is sometimes not recognized, American educational history is a central component of our past. It reflects both our stunning successes as well as our most dramatic failures as a nation. It has provided us with great hope for the future, but also it has been criticized as one of our greatest disappointments. It is one of America's most enduring enigmas.

Like all histories (political, social, economic etc.), the U.S. educational past can be understood through several important lenses or perspectives. Each of these provides us with essential insights as to the progress and failure of what Horace Mann called "the greatest social experiment in history."

THE CHRONOLOGICAL APPROACH

The most common approach we use to understand American educational history is chronological. We begin this story with the Puritan experiment in "universal education," proceed to the emergence of the common school movement of the early nineteenth century, and then to the shift of control of schools from the local community to the state.

The story then continues with the creation of the educational ladder with elementary schools, high schools, and universities, through the twentieth century's progressive experiments, to the testing mania of the late twentieth century, and finally to the growing debate over the efficacy of the public school itself.

IMPORTANCE AND LIMITATIONS OF THE CHRONOLOGICAL APPROACH

The chronological approach is important and places the development of education into a familiar format used by historians for many years. It expresses a kind of linear development in which events seem to follow a prescribed and determined course.

The problem, however, is that the chronological focus can be misleading. History does not unfold in a linear fashion and certainly is not determined or prescribed. Moreover, this approach does not give us a sense of how change happens, the external forces that foster change, or the individuals who implement it. It simply chronicles the events of the past.

THE THEMATIC APPROACH

A useful variation on the chronological approach is to focus on themes in American educational history within a chronological framework. Using this approach, we can examine the changing structure and organization of schools, the consolidation movement, the ongoing struggle for diversity and inclusion, the changes in curriculum and instruction, discipline and moral education, as well as the emergence of testing and assessment of both students and teachers.

While important, this approach is, at its heart, simply a more comprehensive chronicle of educational change. It does not explain educational change fully and certainly does not give us a sense of how education will unfold in the future.

THE TRANSITIONAL APPROACH

One approach that we have found useful is to examine transitions in our educational history. In our *Transitions in American Education*, we centered our attention on the broad macro-changes in American society, economy, and politics and examined how these changes affected American education. We found that there were three distinct transitions in American educational history.

THE FIRST EDUCATIONAL TRANSITION

The first transition was triggered by the American political and constitutional revolutions of the late 1700s coupled with the Market Revolution of the early 1800s. This transition spawned the democratic, locally controlled common school movement. It also promoted a pan-Protestant, virtue-centered curriculum and an instructional model that included memorization and recitation in a competitive environment—such as spelling bees and math contests.

THE SECOND EDUCATIONAL TRANSITION

The urban, corporate, modernization transition followed in the mid- to late nineteenth century and fostered the emergence of state control of education, the graded school, the high school, as well as an instructional movement that emphasized understanding rather than simple memorization.

THE LATEST EDUCATIONAL TRANSITION

The latest educational transition began in the mid-1970s. This demographic, communication, and governmental transition has led to dramatic changes in education including growing federal influence; an instructional focus that centers on comprehension, application, and competency assessed through standardized instruments; as well as the continuing challenges of diversity and segregation within the school-age population.

The theory that underlies the transitional approach to understand educational history is simple. As our nation's social structure becomes more complex, as our political system changes, and as our economy grows and diversifies, we demand new approaches to education.

As demand for change grows, we eventually reach a critical reassessment of our system and education eventually adapts to those new social, political, and economic realities. Eventually we reach a kind of stasis or educational consensus until the next transition.

LIMITATIONS OF THE TRANSITIONAL APPROACH

While this approach is useful, it has two flaws. First, it is abstract and theoretical and focuses on the effect of macro-forces such as demographic changes, political developments, and economic considerations.

Second, with this approach education is reactive rather than causal. It perceives change as a response to external forces, while the causal role of human agency (that is, what people do) essentially is ignored.

CRITICAL MOMENTS OF CHANGE AND THE MEN AND WOMEN WHO MADE THEM

This brings us to *Ten Days That Shook the World of Education*. Here we have focused on the critical moments of change set into motion by everyday people challenging the interlocking injustices of our world to facilitate educational change.

Ten Days is in some ways a synthesis of other approaches we have discussed earlier. It has a chronological component in that it centers on the important moments when change occurs. It also helps us understand the thematic elements of educational change and it demonstrates how individuals reacted to the dramatic macro-changes in American history.

ROUSSEAU, LANCASTER, AND WILLARD

Rousseau, for example, challenged the age-old power of the church and demanded a new approach to both instruction and discipline. Joseph Lancaster, on the other hand, recognized the need to educate the most vulnerable in the new industrial order: the children of the laboring poor. Emma Willard challenged the injustices of gender inequality and successfully promoted the idea of equality of classical education for women as well as the need for formal teacher training.

HORACE MANN

Horace Mann, son of a poor farmer, embraced the great reforms of the mid-nineteenth century and demanded that public education become a central component of that movement. By demanding a secular common school that centered on basic education and an appreciation of diversity and love of country, he propelled education into the modern age.

WILLIAM MCGUFFEY

William McGuffey in many ways made the common school possible through the publication of his *Readers* beginning in the 1830s. These books reinforced the fundamental idea of the common school and helped provide a standardized approach to education that changed the way teachers taught and students learned.

JOHN DEWEY

John Dewey, on the other hand, provided educators with a model of progressive, child-centered education. His lab school at the University of Chicago challenged both the pedagogy and disciplinary approaches of the nineteenth century and provided a link between the early reformers such as Pestalozzi and Rousseau and the neoprogressives of the 1960s and beyond. His innovative methods focused on the importance of democracy and community interdependency and have been a guiding educational force for over a century.

W. E. B. DU BOIS

W. E. B. Du Bois confronted the overt racism of American society and was the first to demand equality of educational opportunities for African Americans. His rejection of universal vocational tracking for black people and his persistent activism propelled education into the mainstream of the civil rights movement. In addition, his role in establishing the NAACP that led the struggle to end legal segregation of public schools in the United States places Du Bois in the pantheon of great educators.

HORACE MANN BOND

Horace Mann Bond built on the work of W. E. B. Du Bois and, as a young man, still in graduate school, challenged the juggernaught of standardized tests, the inherent racial biases in these instruments, and their underlying pernicious philosophy of eugenics. Horace Mann Bond's brilliant career as a scholar, teacher, and administrator was highlighted by a continued struggle against the inherent racism as it applied to African American education.

THURGOOD MARSHALL

Thurgood Marshall in some ways completed the work of Du Bois and Bond. His lifelong activism in the NAACP helped to open the doors of law schools throughout the country and then challenged the legal basis of segregation of American schools in *Brown v. the Board of Education*. Marshall was an untiring progressive who understood the inherent racism of the nation and fought to change society through open and equal education for African Americans.

THE KIDS OF PARKLAND

Finally, we come to "the kids of Parkland," who reopened a chapter of student activism in American educational history. Building on the work of thousands of anonymous students from the past who challenged corporal punishment and outdated policies of *in loco parentis*, the kids of Parkland fearlessly defied local, state, and federal lawmakers and the lobbyists who supported them to put an end to gun violence in schools.

The role of students themselves in educational change is often overlooked by historians. Nevertheless, like philosophers, teachers, and educational activists, they too collectively "shook the world of education."

TWO HUNDRED AND FIFTY YEARS

Our story is nearly complete. We have traveled through over two hundred and fifty years of educational history from Rousseau's two seminal works promoting new approaches to education in the late eighteenth century through the nineteenth, twentieth, and twenty-first centuries when the injustices of classism, gender discrimination, nativism, racism, and school violence were challenged. Throughout this odyssey, education has been the quiet centerpiece of our past.

As we move further into the twenty-first century, we can learn the lessons of these ordinary men and women who faced injustice and shook the world of education. The lessons they provided us will act as a paradigm to improve education in the future.

References

Appiah, K. A. 2014. *Lines of Descent: W. E. B. Du Bois and the Emergence of Identity.* Cambridge, MA: Harvard University Press.
Ball, H. 1998. *A Defiant Life: Thurgood Marshall and the Persistence of Racism in America.* New York: Crown Publications.
Baym, N. 1991. "Women and the Republic: Emma Willard's Rhetoric of History." *American Quarterly* 4 (1): 1–23.
Baynton, D. 2016. *Defectives in the Land: Disability and Immigration in the Age of Eugenics.* Chicago: University of Chicago Press.
Binet, A. *L'Étude expérimentale de l'intelligence.* 1903. (Available through Walmart).
Bond, H. M. 1924. "Intelligence Testing and Propaganda." In *The Crisis Reader: Stories, Poetry, and Essays from the NAACP's Magazine*, edited by Sondra Katherine Wilson. New York: Modern Library.
Bond, H. M. July 1924. "What the Army Intelligence Tests Measured." *Opportunity.*
Bond, H. June 1925. "Temperament." In *The Crisis Reader: Stories, Poetry, and Essays from the NAACP's Magazine*, edited by Sondra Katherine Wilson, 377–84. New York: Modern Library.
Bond, H. M. 1958. "Cat on a Hot Tin Roof." *Journal of Negro Education* 27 (4): 519–25.
Brigham, C. 2017. *A Study of American Intelligence.* New York: Andesite Press.
Burton, W. 1852. *The District School as It Was.* Boston: P. R. Marvin.
Calhoun, D. 1984. "Eyes for the Jacksonian World: William C. Woodbridge and Emma Willard." *Journal of the Early Republic* 4: 1–26.
Caton, J. 2018. *Biographical Sketch of John Dean Caton.* Edited by Robert Fergus. London: in the Forgotten Books.
Cremin, L. 1982. *American Education: The National Experience.* New York: Harper and Row.
Cubberley, E. P. 1919. *Public Education in the United States.* Boston: Houghton, Mifflin and Co.
Curti, M. 1935. *The Social Ideas of American Educators.* New York: Charles Scribner's Sons.
Damrosh, L. 2007. *Rousseau: Restless Genius.* Boston: Mariner Books.
Dewey, J. 1886, 2019. *Psychology.* New York: Wentworth Press.
Dewey, J. 1889. *Psychology: Introduction to the Principles and Practice of Education. The Early Works of John Dewey, Volume 1 (1882–1898).* Carbondale: Southern Illinois University Press.
Dewey, J. 1902, 2008. *The Child and the Curriculum.* New York: Cosimo Classics.
Dewey, J. 1916. *Democracy and Education: An Introduction to the Philosophy of Education.* New York: Macmillan.
Dewey, J. 1925, 2000. *Experience in Nature.* Mineola, NY: Dover Publications.

Dewey, J. 1929, 1974. *Impressions of Soviet Russia and the Revolutionary World*. New York: Teacher College.
Dewey, J. 1938, 1997. *Experience and Education*. New York: Free Press.
Dewey, J. 1939, 1989. *Freedom and Culture*. Amherst, NY: Prometheus.
Dewey, J., and E. Dewey. 1915. *Schools of To-Morrow*. New York: E. P. Dutton and Co.
Du Bois, W. E. B. 1897, 2014. *The Philadelphia Negro*. Oxford: Oxford University Press.
Du Bois, W. E. B. 1903, 2016. *The Soul of Black Folk*. Mineola, NY: Dover Publications.
Everytown for Gun Safety. 2019. *Report: Protecting Kids and Our Communities*. November 11.
Finkelstein, B. 1989. *Governing the Young: Teacher Behavior in Popular Primary Schools in Nineteenth Century United States*. New York: Falmer Press.
Gibson, L. 2012. *Young Thurgood: The Making of a Supreme Court Justice*. Amherst, NY: Prometheus Books.
Goddard, H. 1912, 2008. *The Kallikak Family*. Scotts Valley, CA: Create Space Independent Publishing Platform.
Hewitt, E. 1884. *A Treatise on Pedagogy for Young Teachers*. Cincinnati: Van Antwerp, Bragg and Co.
Hogan, David. 1989. "The Market Revolution and Disciplinary Power: Joseph Lancaster and the Psychology of the Early Classroom System." *History of Education Quarterly* 29 (3): 381–417.
Holy Bible. Proverbs 23:13–14.
Horne, G. 2010. *W. E. B. Du Bois: A Biography*. Westport, CT: Greenwood Press.
Johnson, B. 2008. *W. E. B. Du Bois: Toward Agnosticism 1865–1934*. Lanham, MA: Rowman & Littlefield.
Kennedy, D. 1980. *Over There: The First World War in American Society*. New York: Oxford University Press.
Kaestle, C. 1973. *Joseph Lancaster and the Monitorial School Movement*. New York: Teachers College Press.
Kevles, D. 1985. *In the Name of Eugenics*. Cambridge, MA: Harvard University Press.
Kluger, R. 2004. *Simple Justice: The History of Brown v Board of Education and Black America's Struggle for Equality*. New York: Vintage Books.
Knoll, M. "John Dewey as Administrator: The Inglorious End of the Laboratory School in Chicago." *Journal of Curriculum Studies* 47 (April): 203–52.
Lancaster, J. 1803. *Improvements in Education*. London: Darton and Harvey.
Lancaster, J. 1833. *The Epitome of the Chief Events and Transactions of my own Life*. New Haven, CT: n.p.
Lewis, D. L. 1993. *W. E. B. Du Bois: A Biography of a Race, 1868–1919*. New York: Henry Holt and Co.
Lewis, D. L. 2009. *W. E. B. Du Bois: The Fight for Equality and the American Century 1919–1963*. New York: Holt Paperbacks.
Locke, J. 1705, 1968. *Some Thoughts Concerning Education in the Educational Writings of John Locke*. Edited by James Axtell, 110–325. Cambridge: Cambridge University Press.
Lutz, A. 1964. *Pioneer Educator of American Women*. Boston: Beacon Press.
McGuffey, W. H. 1836, 1982. *McGuffeys Eclectic Readers Series*. Fenton, MI: Mott Media.
McGrew, Jaime C., ed. 2015. *Booker T. Washington and W. E. B. Du Bois: Two Speeches and an Essay*. Scotts Valley, CA: Create Space Independent Platform.
Martin, J. 2003. *The Education of John Dewey*. New York: Columbia University Press.
Mann, H. 1846. *Report of the Educational Tour in Germany*. London: n.p.
Mann, M. B. 1937. *Life of Horace Mann*. Washington, DC: National Education Association.
Messerli, J. 1972. *Horace Mann: A Biography*. New York: Alfred A. Knopf.
Mosier, R. 1965. *Making the American Mind: Social and Moral Ideas in the McGuffey Readers*. New York: Russell and Russell Publications.
Murphy, M. 1990. *Blackboard Unions: The AFT and the NEA, 1900–1980*. Ithaca, NY: Cornell University Press.
Northend, C. 1853. *The Teacher and the Parent: Treatise Upon School Education, Containing Practical Suggestions to Teachers and Parents*. Boston: Jenks, Hickling and Swan.

Page, D. 1867. *Theory and Practice of Teaching.* New York: American Book Co.
Parkerson, D., and J. Parkerson J. 2001. *Transitions in American Education: A Social History of Teaching.* New York: RoutledgeFalmer.
Potter, A. 1842. *The School and the Schoolmaster: A Manual for the Use of Teachers, Employers, Trustees, Inspectors, Etc., of Common Schools, Pt. 1.* New York: Harper and Brothers.
Ray, Joseph. 1800s, 2001. *Ray's Arithmetic Series.* 8 volumes. Fenton, MI: Mott Media.
Reese, J. L. 1827. *A Pocket Manual of the Lancastrian's Method of Education in Its Most Improved State as Practical in the Modern School.* Philadelphia: n.p.
Rousseau, J. 1762, 1968. *The Social Contract of Principles of Political Right.* London: Penguin Classics.
Rousseau, J. 1762, 1974. *Emile or on Education.* Translated by Barbara Foxley. London: Everyman's Library.
Rudwick, Elliott. 1969. *The Making of Black America, Volume II: The Black Community in Black America.* New York: Atheneum.
Ruggles, A. 1950. *The Story of the McGuffeys.* Woodstock, GA: American Book Co.
Salmon, D. 1904. *Joseph Lancaster.* London: Longmans, Green and Co.
Shuey, A. 1958. *The Testing of Negro Intelligence.* New York: Social Science Press.
Taylor, B. 2010. *Horace Mann's Legacy: The Education of Democratic Citizens.* Lawrence: University Press of Kansas.
Urban, W. 2008. *Black Scholar: Horace Mann Bond, 1904–1972.* Athens: University of Georgia.
Westbrook, R. 1992. "John Dewey and American Democracy." *American Historical Review* 97 (3): 919–20.
Westbrook, R. 1993. *John Dewey and American Democracy.* Ithaca, NY: Cornell University Press.
Willard, E. 1819, 2019. *An Address to the Public: Particularly to the Members of the Legislature of New York Proposing a Plan for Improving Female Education.* Sydney, Australia: Wentworth Press.

About the Authors

Donald Parkerson is distinguished professor of teaching in the Department of History at East Carolina University. He has published seven books on the history of education with his coauthor, Jo Ann Parkerson. Their previous books with Rowman & Littlefield were *The Struggle for Public Education* and *Assessment, Bureaucracy and Consolidation*.

Jo Ann Parkerson is professor emeritus of education at Methodist University. In addition to publishing seven books on educational history with Donald Parkerson, she has published articles in the *Journal of Educational Psychology* and *Evaluation in Education: An International Review*. Previously, she taught in the public schools and she draws upon her educational experiences and research in her writing.

www.ingramcontent.com/pod-product-compliance
Lightning Source LLC
Chambersburg PA
CBHW052047300426
44117CB00012B/2004